CONCURRENT PROGRAMMING
for software engineers

'1

ELLIS HORWOOD BOOKS IN COMPUTING SCIENCE
General Editors: Professor JOHN CAMPBELL, University College London, and BRIAN L. MEEK, King's College London (KQC), University of London

Series in Computers and their Applications
Series Editor: BRIAN L. MEEK, Computer Centre, King's College London (KQC), University of London
An up-to-date and readable list of texts on the theory and practice of computing, with the emphasis on computer applications and new or developing areas: a valuable nucleus for all computing science libraries and departments.

Series in Computer Communications and Networking
Series Editor: R. J. DEASINGTON, International Computers Limited (UK), Edinburgh
Books covering an area of growing current interest in data communications technology, local area networks (LANs) and wide area networks (WANs); aimed at both professional users of network and communication systems, as well as academics.

Series in Artificial Intelligence
Series Editor: Professor JOHN CAMPBELL, University College London
Books which reflect the latest and most important developments in the field of Artificial Intelligence, edited by a most prestigious and well respected authority of world renown.

Series in Cognitive Science
Series Editor: MASOUD YAZDANI, Department of Computer Science, University of Exeter
A series which reports on work being carried out in an emerging discipline, an area of artificial intelligence which is being recognised as an independent study in its own right.

ELLIS HORWOOD BOOKS IN INFORMATION TECHNOLOGY
General Editor: Dr JOHN M. M. PINKERTON, Principal, McLean Pinkerton Associates, Surrey (formerly General Manager of Strategic Requirements, ICL)
Books are planned in this area in knowledge engineering, expert systems, the human–computer interface, computational linguistics; and will cover the many applications of information technology.

If you would like more information on titles in any of these areas, please contact our distributors and ask them for a catalogue of our publications.

JOHN WILEY & SONS LTD
Baffins Lane
Chichester
West Sussex
England

Halsted Press: a division of
JOHN WILEY & SONS, INC
605 Third Avenue
New York, NY 10158
USA

CONCURRENT PROGRAMMING
for software engineers

DICK WHIDDETT, B.Sc., M.A., Ph.D.
Head of Micro Unit, Department of Computing
University of Lancaster

ELLIS HORWOOD LIMITED
Publishers · Chichester

Halsted Press: a division of
JOHN WILEY & SONS
New York · Chichester · Brisbane · Toronto

First published in 1987 by
ELLIS HORWOOD LIMITED
Market Cross House, Cooper Street,
Chichester, West Sussex, PO19 1EB, England
The publisher's colophon is reproduced from James Gillison's drawing of the ancient Market Cross, Chichester.

Distributors:

Australia and New Zealand:
JACARANDA WILEY LIMITED
GPO Box 859, Brisbane, Queensland 4001, Australia

Canada:
JOHN WILEY & SONS CANADA LIMITED
22 Worcester Road, Rexdale, Ontario, Canada

Europe and Africa:
JOHN WILEY & SONS LIMITED
Baffins Lane, Chichester, West Sussex, England

North and South America and the rest of the world:
Halsted Press: a division of
JOHN WILEY & SONS
605 Third Avenue, New York, NY 10158, USA

© 1987 R. J. Whiddett/Ellis Horwood Limited

British Library Cataloguing in Publication Data
Whiddett, R. J.
Concurrent programming for software engineers. —
(Computers and their applications).
1. Parallel processing (Electronic computers)
2. Operating systems (computers)
I. Title   II. Series
005.4′2   QA76.6

Library of Congress CIP data available

ISBN 0–7458–0036–X (Ellis Horwood Limited — Library Edition)
ISBN 0–7458–0338–5 (Ellis Horwood Limited — Student Edition)
ISBN 0–470–20979–8 (Halsted Press)

Printed in Great Britain by R. J. Acford, Chichester

Contents

PART II - THE MODELS

Preface

This book aims to introduce the most important aspects of concurrent programming which have been developed for use on traditional architecture computers. It concentrates on high-level language features that have evolved and considers the underlying implementation techniques.

Concurrent programming and the use of high-level languages are very important for the implementation of complex real-time control systems. Their importance is now being recognised for the programming of microprocessor based systems. Concurrent programming tools were first developed in the context of complex computer operating systems. Thus concurrent programming is traditionally taught as a component of operating systems courses in computer science and rarely to engineers. Consequently there is a need for a text which covers all aspects of concurrent programming techniques and is not oriented to operating systems applications.

The three basic paradigms of concurrent programming that are currently subjects of active research are examined, i.e. monitor, message and operation oriented systems. The use of each of these three paradigms is demonstrated by the development of designs for two systems, a data-logger and a carpark controller. These designs illustrate the relative strengths and weaknesses of the three approaches.

The final section of the book considers aspects of system implementations; the underlying techniques of process implementation and control; the interface to peripheral devices and hardware interrupts; and finally the programming of distributed systems.

The book is relevant to engineers, students, teachers and researchers in all aspects of digital electronics, information technology and computer systems.

To my parents.

Acknowledgements

I would like to extend my thanks my collegues at Lancaster for their help and support in this venture, especially to John Gallagher for his patient and pains-taking reviews and criticisms of the early drafts, and to Craig Wiley and Gordon Blair for their comments on the later drafts. Thanks also to Brian Meek, the series editor, for his review and useful comments.

To Liz Rowley and Maxine Robinson for their work in preparing the manuscript.

And to Jocelyn, for being so absorbed in writing her own book that she did not notice that I was ignoring her.

PART I

The Basics

This first part of the book introduces the basic ideas of a process. Chapter 1 introduces high-level languages and some aspects of implementing a program as a single process. Chapter 2 introduces some of the problems that emerge when independent processes attempt to co-ordinate their action.

1

The Concept of a Process

1.1. INTRODUCTION

There has been a great expansion in the development of multi-processors and the use of computers in control systems since the introduction of microprocessor technologies. The programming of these systems requires the special facilities provided by concurrent programming languages; which in turn has intensified the investigation of methods of representing and implementing such concurrency. This book aims to examine the most important of these developments.

Currently, the most important applications of concurrent programming techniques are in the areas of real-time control systems and operating systems implementations. These programs need to be able to represent the apparent simultaneous operation of several devices such as machines or peripheral devices. Because these devices interact with the external environment, the computer does not have strict control over the sequence in which events occur. A concurrent language therefore needs to be able to provide for the non-deterministic operation of a program which is synchronised with the the external environment.

This contrasts with the vast majority of programs which are sequential in nature. A sequential program defines a sequence of operations to be performed on some data. At each stage of a program's execution the sequence in which the operations will be performed is determined solely by the program and the data values. Repeated execution of the same program with the same data should produce the same results irrespective of the exact time or speed of the program's execution. It is precisely for these reasons that computers are entrusted with jobs such as calculating salaries or designing cars.

Typical sequential programming languages, such as Fortran, Basic and Pascal, consist of sequences of statements which are generally executed in the order in which they are written. Special language features are used to introduce the conditional or repetitive execution of some statements and to group sequences of statements into procedures or subroutines.

Concurrent programs are usually implemented as a collection of processes, where a process roughly corresponds with the idea of the execution of a sequential program. Therefore, the reader should have a sound grasp of sequential programming before moving on to consider concurrency. Most of the developments in concurrent techniques have taken place since the early seventies and have either been based on the language Pascal or have been very heavily influenced by it; thus a knowledge or familiarity with this language will be useful for the reader.

One aim of this book is to provide an understanding of how the higher-level features of the languages are actually implemented on the underlying hardware. This understanding is useful since the application areas of concurrent languages are not as divorced from the hardware as are other applications, and an understanding of the entire 'computer system' is sometimes necessary. Furthermore, it may prove necessary for a programmer or engineer to modify the actual language implementation to meet specific requirements, such as timing constraints. In this case an understanding of the relationship between the program source code and the resulting machine code is essential. Concurrent languages are still relatively immature and are not as effective as sequential languages at 'hiding the machine' from the programmer. It is therefore useful to see why things are done in particular ways and how the language design is influenced by the underlying hardware.

The book is composed of three parts. Potential readers of this book may have very diverse backgrounds depending on whether they are 'programmers', or are 'engineers' with limited exposure to high level languages. To cater for this potential deficiency this chapter begins by providing the foundations of high-level programming concepts and their implementation. It then proceeds to explain how multiple processes may be implemented on a single hardware processor. Chapter 2 develops the ideas of using multiple processes and introduces the concepts and problems associated with their interaction and cooperation.

The second part of the book is concerned with the refinements of language features to represent the interactions between processes. Three chapters each examine separate major paradigms. These paradigms feature shared data or monitors; message exchange; and finally systems based on active objects which may be considered to fall part way between the first two paradigms. Chapter 6 draws the three themes together by comparing the relative merits of the various techniques.

The final part of the book is concerned with the pragmatics of implementing computer systems. Chapter 7 considers techniques which have been used to provide the interface between the program, the processor and peripheral devices, an area of particular relevance when using microprocessors as control elements embedded within larger systems. The final chapter examines the programming of distributed computer systems, i.e. systems with several processors but no common memory. Systems with this architecture have great economic and technical appeal but are still under-exploited. The reasons for their relative under-development lie in the problems involved in implementing adequate software. The chapter focuses on the ways in which the different programming paradigms of monitors, messages and operations may be mapped onto distributed systems.

The book concentrates on practical systems throughout. It is therefore concerned with the programming of computers with traditional processor architectures using traditional 'process oriented' languages. The use of alternative architecture computers and 'data flow' programs are beyond the scope of this text. The interested reader is referred to the book by Bishop (1986) for an introduction to alternative architectures.

1.2. SEQUENTIAL PROGRAM STRUCTURES

The science of programming language design came of age only with the definition of Algol-60. These design techniques were refined over the following years, so that when Niklaus Wirth developed the language Pascal (Jensen, 1975) in 1969 the result was an elegant, useful language. Pascal is a coherent language with few special cases or ad-hoc restrictions and a wide range of powerful useful features. These attributes make it very popular with both programmers and language implementors. As a result Pascal has strongly influenced the subsequent evolution of programming language design in general and concurrent languages in particular.

Before embarking on concurrent programming the reader should be familiar and competent in the use of a sequential programming language, preferably Pascal or a related language. It is outside the scope of this book to provide an introduction to programming or language design. This section will emphasise some of the points of design and implementation required later in the book. A more detailed study of aspects of language design, particularly related to real-time languages, may be found in the book by S.J. Young (1982).

This book will follow the usual convention of representing the 'reserved words' or 'keywords' of programming languages in bold typeface, for example, **begin** and **end;** other words and symbols are represented in italic font, for example, *total* and *integer*.

1.2.1. Types, variables and references

A principal design feature of most computers is flexibility; in particular, flexibility in storing or manipulating programs and data in the main memory. Unfortunately, this flexibility can lead to problems in the test and implementation phases of program development since it makes error tracing very difficult. Some processors ease the problem slightly by 'partitioning' the memory into program and data areas, which at least, prevents the program from being corrupted. However, very few hardware systems provide any support in controlling the way in which data is manipulated. The processor has no way of determining from the hardware the form of the information in a memory location. This information may be used to represent an integer, a character or a real number. Consequently there is no way for the processor to determine the validity of the operations it performs and it will readily perform nonsensical operations on request, such as adding together integers and characters. High-level languages attempt to prevent erroneous operations by carefully controlling the generation and execution of program instructions. However, the use of high-level languages and compilers does not actually prohibit the hardware from performing nonsensical operations.

A compiler provides this protection by formalising the concept of data types. High level languages require the programmer to specify, or declare, the names of all program variables to be used, together with the type of data that they each represent. Early languages provided only a few basic data types, such as integer and real numbers, and restricted the operations that could be performed on them. Pascal and later languages provide additional basic types and allow the user to define new types or subtypes. This refines the degree to which the compiler can check a program for logical correctness. Once a new type has been defined, variables of that type may be declared.

The strictness of the rules defining the legality of operations is referred to as the 'strength' of the type checking. Strict rules give a 'strongly typed' language whilst more liberal rules are 'weak'. Strongly typed languages give the user greater protection since many errors may be detected by the compiler. Compilers for strongly typed languages may also generate instructions to check the use of data during the program's execution, which aids the detection of program faults. It is argued that because of these advantages, strongly typed languages lead to better designed, more reliable and more testable software, as well as providing greater programmer productivity overall.

Proponents of weakly typed languages claim that strong typing is over-restrictive and leads to inefficient designs. With the notable exception of the C language (Kernighan, 1978) most modern languages are quite strongly typed.

As well as providing basic types such as integers and characters, many languages allow the definition of 'subranges' of these types which may be used to represent a restricted range of values. For instance the type-definition:-

> *percent = 0..100*

introduces a new variable type called *percent*. Variables of this type will be restricted to retaining a value in the defined range.

New variable types may also be introduced as user-defined scalar types. For example, the definition:-

> *colour = (red, blue, green)*

introduces a new variable type which may only be set to one of the defined values. Few operations are defined for user-defined scalar-types, but they prove useful in enhancing the readability of programs.

Once a new types has been defined, data variables may be declared, giving their names and types in the usual manner. For example:-

```
i          : integer;
c1, c2    : char;
hue       : colour;
discount : percent;
inflation : 0..1000;
```

The above definition of the variable *inflation* is a contracted form which combines the declaration of a variable with a definition of its type.

The type and memory requirements of each variable are known to the compiler, which may allocate a suitable memory area to represent the variable during the .program's execution. The actual memory addresses that are used are generally of no interest to the programmer who usually refers to variables by their names.

Since the compiler knows the types of all program variables it can detect many program errors arising from to the inappropriate use of variables, such as adding a character variable to an integer. These errors are known as 'type conflicts'. Some type conflicts are less serious and the compiler may automatically generate code to convert a variable of one type to another. For example, it may convert integers to real numbers if necessary. This process is called 'coercion'. Some languages, such as Algol-68, provide extensive automatic coercions; others, such as Ada, do not provide any automatically, but allow the user to request individual coercions to be applied.

Some errors cannot be detected on compilation since they may depend on the actual values of variables which are known only when the program is executed. In such cases the compiler usually generates additional instructions to check that the result is acceptable. For example, the first statement in the following program would cause a compilation error and the second would produce an error on execution since *pos* is constrained to values between 1 and 100.

type
> *position = 1..100;*

var
> *pos : position;*

begin
> *pos := "C";*
> *pos := 100+1*

end

Since the compiler takes care of all address allocation, the programmer cannot manipulate variables using their addresses nor can he store an address for later use. These operations are very useful for manipulating variable lengthed lists or other complex data structures. Address manipulation is usually incorporated into a language using a 'reference' or 'pointer' variable. These variables are declared like normal data variables, but the only values that may be assigned to them are addresses of variables of a particular type. For example, if *pti* is declared to be a pointer to an integer, it could only ever refer to an integer variable. Attempts to assign to *pti* the address of a variable of type real, or an integer value, such as 5, would not be accepted by the compiler.

Most languages define a very restricted range of operations which manipulate pointers or references; usually the programmer is restricted to assigning values to them or testing whether two pointers refer to the same object. A pointer may also be 'dereference' to allow the manipulation of the object to which it refers. In Pascal this is represented by following the pointer name by an up-arrow character (↑); thus if the variable *pti* points to some integer variable, the statement:-

> *pti*↑ := 5

would assign the value of 5 to that integer variable, the value of *pti* itself would be unaffected.

A special value, *nil*, is defined for all pointer types which corresponds to zero in numerical types. A pointer of value *nil* does not reference any object. Dereferencing a *nil* pointer leads to an execution error. For example:-

> *pti := nil;*
> *pti*↑ := 5

would cause an error on execution.

Pointers are used extensively in the implementation of operating systems and concurrent languages. Readers unfamiliar with their use can find more details and examples in Appendix A.

The use of pointer types has proved most useful and most modern hardware supports their implementation with some form of address indirection operations.

All of the individual variables discussed in this section are capable of storing only one value at a time. These are referred to as 'simple types'. The next section covers the more sophisticated 'structured types'.

1.2.2. Structured types

Simple variables only provide storage of one value, but it is often useful to group collections of related variables together to simplify the logic of a program and also to make it more efficient. The groupings are provided by 'structured' types. Specific varieties of structured types can be defined and the definitions used to declare structured variables. The two most common varieties of structured types are arrays and records.

Arrays provide groupings of items of the same component type. An array normally has provision to store a fixed number of elements. Individual elements do not have their own name but are referenced by an 'index' specifying their position in the array. The range of the index is specified in the array's type definition and defines its size. The range is usually specified by giving the lower and upper bounds of the index. Many modern languages allow the range to be specified by any scalar type. Some more primitive languages restrict the range to integer values and some even specify a value for the lower bounds, which is usually defined to be 0 or 1. The following examples each declare array types containing 3 elements:-

arraytype1 = **array**[*-1..1*] **of** *integer;*
arraytype2 = **array**[*1..3*] **of** *real;*

colour   = *(red, blue, green);*
arraytype3 = **array**[*colour*] **of** *boolean;*

Once the form of an array type has been defined in a type definition, a number of instances may be declared as named variables. The contracted form of variable declaration is often allowed with arrays; however, in a very strongly typed language this may restrict the utility of the resulting variable. To manipulate the elements of an array it is necessary to specify both the array name and the element's index, which is usually enclosed in square brackets. The following example uses the type definitions given above to declare and use some variables:-

    var
        array1 : arraytype1;
        array3 : arraytype3;
        array4 : **array**[*-1..1*] **of** *integer;*

```
begin
        array1[0]        := 5;
        array4[0]        := array1[0];
        array3[blue]     := true
end
```

The component types of arrays are not usually restricted to simple types. Arrays of structured types are often permitted. Thus multi-dimensional arrays may be implemented using arrays of arrays, if they are not permitted directly in the language.

The two methods commonly used to implement array storage and access are illustrated in Fig. 1.1. In the first method the array elements may be allocated sequential memory locations, in which case the ith element may be accessed by multiplying i by the element size and adding this offset to the address of the beginning of the array. The details of the language rules determine whether the size of the array elements may be determined during compilation and inserted as a constant into the program code or whether their size may vary, in which case the size of the elements must be stored with the array itself and determined during the program's execution.

An alternative implementation technique is to store an array of references which are initialised to give the addresses of the actual elements of the program's array. The elements of the program's array are stored elsewhere. The ith element of the program's array may be accessed by first adding i to the base address of the array of addresses to obtain the address (say j) of the ith element of this array. Next j may be used to retrieve the program array's element's address (say k). Finally, k may then be used to access the contents of the program's variable. The overhead of the extra memory used to contain the references may be justified in terms of execution speed, since it avoids a multiplication operation which may be very slow on some machines.

Arrays provide the mechanism for encapsulating collections of similar items; however, to encapsulate variables of differing types a record must be used. A record consists of a fixed number of components called 'fields'. The fields are not indexed as arrays are, but each field is named by a field-identifier. A record type-definition begins and ends with some key-word identifier and consist of a series of field-identifiers and their types. Field types are not restricted to simple types but may be structured types, such as arrays and records. For instance the following record might be used to represent a car:-

```
car =    record
                make, model      : array[1..10] of char;
                enginesize       : integer;
                shade            : colour;
        end
```

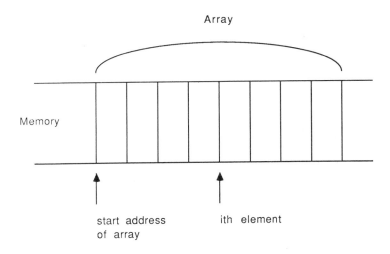

Method 1: Contiguous locations.

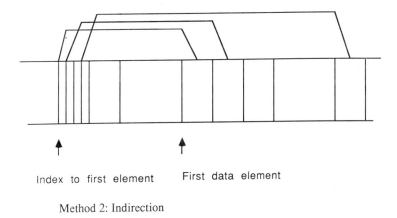

Method 2: Indirection

Fig. 1.1 - Implementations of Arrays.

The fields of the record may be selected by first selecting the record variable's name and appending a field-identifier, usually connecting them with a full-stop. For example, given a variable *mycar* of type *car* some fields could be set as follows:-

> *mycar.enginesize := 1600;*
> *mycar.shade   := blue;*

Programs often require a number of similar record types with only slightly varied definitions. For example, records may be required to describe vans and coaches giving either their maximum load or seating capacity. One solution would be to include all the fields in all records and ignore those that are not relevant. This solution may waste a lot of memory since space is reserved for all fields whether or not they are used. The problem is overcome by 'variant records' which define a range of related record structures. The variant record definition begins with the definition of fields common to all varieties. These are followed by a special field called the 'tag' or 'discriminant' field which is a scalar value defining the particular form of the rest of the structure. This is followed by a definition of the fields which are present for the possible values of the tag field. For example, various kinds of motor vehicle could be described by the record:-

> *vehicle_kind = (van, coach, car);*

> *vehicle =*   **record**
>   *make, model*   : **array[1..10] of** *char;*
>   *enginesize*   : *integer;*
>   *shade*   : *colour;*
>   *reg*   : **array[1..7] of** *char;*
>   **case** *kind*   : *vehicle_kind* **of**
>   *van*   : *(max_load*   : *integer);*
>   *coach*   : *(seats*   : *integer);*
>   *car*   : *()*
>   **end** {*of case and record*}

In this example the tag field *kind* is a scalar with three possible values so there are three possible variants. The *car* variant has no additional fields, whilst the other two have one field each. Although this example only shows one field per variant there is no limit to the number of such fields. When a variant record variable is declared the default action is to reserve space for the largest possible variant. However, if the value of the tag field is specified, space is only reserved for the fields of that variant. Ideally the tag field should be checked before each access to an optional field of a record to ensure the validity of the operation. For instance, if a vehicle record has its *kind* field set to *van* it is an error to access a *seats* field. In practice the same area of memory is used for each variant and the programmer is expected to do any checking necessary. Thus the *max_load* and *seats* fields of a particular record refer to the same memory location. This loophole in the type checking has made variant records a contentious feature of Pascal. The above example is not too serious since the possible values stored in the variant part are of the same type. However, if one field were used to represent a pointer variable it would be possible to generate some very obscure execution errors by treating a data variable as a memory address. Despite the problems of variant records they prove very useful in practice and have been included in Ada as well in as Pascal.

The implementation and use of records is simple in comparison to that of arrays. The declaration of a record variable reserves an appropriate storage area for all the fields which are stored in sequential locations. Sometimes addressing constraints of the hardware means that it is necessary to start fields at particular addresses leaving small gaps of unused memory between some fields. For instance, it may be necessary to store integers at even numbered addresses leaving an odd byte free after a single character field. However, once the memory has been allocated, the selection of fields is straightforward since field names must be expressed as literals in the program and are fixed on compilation. This contrasts with array subscripts, which may be variables whose values are unknown until the program is executed. Fields of records may be accessed directly and efficiently like a simple variable in many cases. Accessing a field from a record that is being indirectly referenced through a pointer variable simply involves adding a fixed offset to the pointer which references the start of the record. For instance, if *ptv* is a variable of type 'pointer to vehicle' which references a record *myvehicle* then the two statements:-

myvehicle.enginesize := 1600

and

ptv↑.enginesize := 1600

would both have the same result. However, the first statement may access the location directly, whereas the second would determine the address to use by adding to the value of *ptv* an offset corresponding to the size of the two arrays of characters preceding *enginesize* in the record.

In addition to those which access individual elements of structured types, some operations may be defined for the complete structures. These are usually assignments and tests of equality. An assignment between a pair of arrays or a pair of records involves setting all of the values of fields in the target variable to the values of the corresponding fields in the source variable. This is may be more efficient than copying each component individually. Thus a program controlling a car assembly line might employ a statement of the form:-

newcar := standard_saloon

or

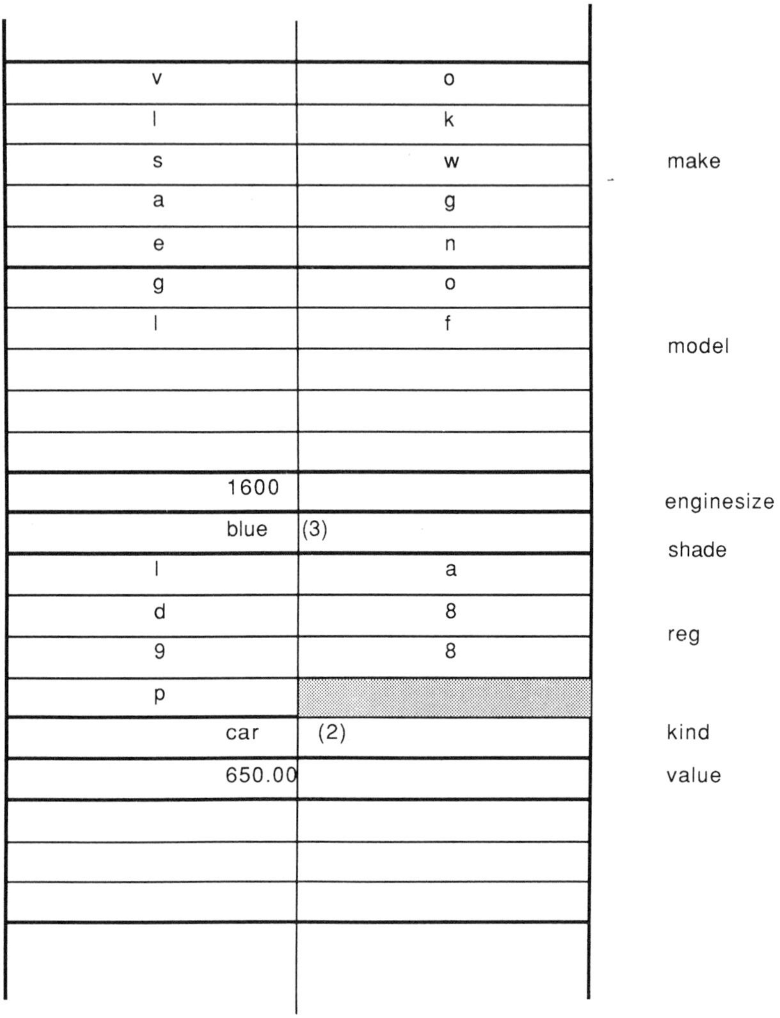

v	o	
l	k	
s	w	make
a	g	
e	n	
g	o	
l	f	
		model
1600		enginesize
blue	(3)	shade
l	a	
d	8	
9	8	reg
p		
car	(2)	kind
650.00		value

Fig. 1.2 - Implementation of a record.

newcar := delux_version

to initialise the record describing a car depending on its variety, where *standard_saloon* and *delux_version* are records initialised to appropriate standard values. The program might then make use of an equality test of the form:-

if *this_car = delux_version* **then** ....

1.2.3. Allocating and accessing variables

The previous sections discussed the ideas of data types and simple and structured variables but did not examine how the variables might be declared or generated. Most strongly typed languages require all variables to be 'declared', giving their name and type, before they may be used. This aids the compiler in type checking. The process of type-checking is usually aided further by limiting the places within a program where declarations are allowed. This contrasts with Fortran or Basic which allow some types of variables to be introduced anywhere in a program without declaring them.

Many languages have developed around the idea of 'blocks', and are called 'block-structured' languages. Blocks provide a mechanism for dividing a program into small sections of manageable size, and they also serve to control the lifetime of program variables. A block structured program consists of a series of individual program blocks or segments which are delineated by some reserved words, such as **declare** and **end** in Ada. Blocks may contain sub-blocks in a recursive manner leading to a 'nested' program structure.

Type definitions and variable declarations are usually restricted to the beginning of a block and are followed by the program statements which manipulate them. During the execution of a program the variables declared at the beginning of a block are allocated space when their block is activated. They disappear on completion of the block. If the block is subsequently re-executed, a completely new set of variables are allocated. The section of program within which a variable is declared is said to be its 'scope'. These ideas are illustrated in the following program extract in Ada. In it the variables a and b exist throughout its execution, but there are ten incarnations of the variables x and y which are repeatedly created and subsequently discarded:-

```
    declare
        a, b: integer;

    begin
            for i in 1..10 loop
                declare
                        x, y : integer;

                begin
                        x := a;
                        ...
                end
            end loop
    end
```

Since the variable a is declared in the outer block it may be accessed from the inner one. In most block-structured languages the default case allows the inner blocks to access any variables declared in enclosing blocks.

Variables in enclosing blocks are said to be 'global' to the enclosed block. It is quite legitimate to use the same variable name in several blocks; they may even declare variables of different types. Any occurrence of the variable name is taken to refer to the variable in the closest enclosing block. The following program demonstrates the application of these rules.

```
declare
        a : integer;

begin
        declare
                x : integer;

        begin
                x := 1;          -- local variable
                a := 1;          -- global variable
        end;

        declare
                a : integer;

        begin
                x := 1;          -- error no global x
                a := 1;          -- local variable
        end;
end
```

In this example the second reference to x would be detected as an error by the compiler since there is no variable named x declared in the current block or in the *enclosing* blocks. Notice also that the second reference to a accesses a local variable rather than the global one. This is effectively redefining the variable and makes the global variable inaccessible. The accidental redefinition of variables in this manner is a common source of program errors, particularly in heavily nested programs, since the resulting program is often quite acceptable to the compiler and no error messages or warnings are generated.

The scope rules of block structured languages are quite simple to understand and implement. However, they have suffered severe criticism for being rather liberal, since variables in the outer blocks may be accessed from so much of the program. Thus some languages, especially concurrent ones, whilst retaining the general block-structure, have added other features to control the accessibility of variables. These features will be considered further in later chapters. The mechanisms used to implement the allocation and access of variables in blocks are considered further in a later section of this chapter.

1.2.4. Program control statements

The previous sections have touched on the language facilities and mechanisms which aid the programmer to define and use different data types. This section will examine the support provided for the specification of the control aspects of a program.

The first requirement is an adequate set of basic constructs to express the conditional and repetitive execution of sequences of statements, and to express the selection of one of a set of options. The details of features provided in various languages differ; the following examples illustrate the facilities provided by Pascal.

Conditional execution is provided by the 'if statement' which has the form:-

> **if** <*expression*> **then** <*statement_1*> **else** <*statement_2*>

The <*expression*> may be of arbitrary complexity provided that it yields a boolean result. If the evaluation of the expression yields a value of *true* then <*statement_1*> is executed and control then proceeds to the following program statement. The '**else** <*statement_2*>' construct is optional. If the <*expression*> yields a result of *false* and an 'else clause' is provided, then <*statement_2*> is executed before control passes to the next statement. The generality of the construct is enhanced in Pascal since the reserved words **begin** and **end** may be used to enclose any number of statements to form a single 'compound statement' which may appear in either branch of the 'if statement'.

Pascal provides three forms of repetitive statement; for, while and repeat. A 'for statement' allows a statement to be executed a fixed number of times while changing the value of a 'control variable' each time. The general form is:-

> **for** <*variable*> := <*expression_1*> **to** <*expression_2*> **do**
>   <*statement*>

The variable is initialised to the value of <*expression_1*> and <*statement*> is executed, the value of the variable is then incremented. While the value of the variable remains less than or equal to <*expression_2*> the <*statement*> is executed and the variable incremented. When the variable exceeds the second expression control is passed to the next statement. 'For statements' are particularly useful in manipulating arrays, for example:-

> **for** *i:= 1* **to** *10* **do**
>   *total := total + A[i]*

adds the first ten elements of *A[i]* to *total*.

The 'while statements' and 'repeat statements' are more flexible. They have the form:-

while *<expression>* **do**
          <statement>

and

repeat
          <statement>
until *<expression>*

The 'while statement' repeated evaluates *<expression>* and if the result is *true* the *<statement>* is executed. Control is passed to the next program statement when the evaluation delivers a result of *false*. In order for control to leave the loop the *<statement>* must perform some action which will change the value of *<expression>*, for example:-

while *i <= 10* **do**
          begin
                    total   := total + A[i];
                    i   := i + 1
          end

The 'repeat statement' follows the same format except that the test is performed after the execution of *<statement>*, meaning that the *<statement>* is executed at least once, which may not be the case with a 'while statement'.

The 'case statement' allows the multi-way selection of statements depending on the value of an expression. The general form is:-

case *<expression>* **of**
          <label_1> : <statement_1>;
          ...
          <label_N> : <statement_N>
end

The *<expression>* must evaluate to yield a scalar value and the statement labelled with the corresponding value is executed before control is passed to the next program statement. An example might be:-

case *cartype* **of**
          standard: enginesize := 1200;
          delux   : enginesize := 2000;
          gti   : enginesize := 3500
end

For a language to be generally useful, the basic statement forms which provide the repetitive and conditional program execution must be complemented by a comprehensive set of mechanisms for accessing data variables and manipulating them in expressions. Ideally the language should allow for any degree of complexity in the evaluation of a component of an expression. The programmer should be able to provide either a simple literal value or invoke any degree of pointer dereferencing, array subscripting or record selection to deliver the requisite value. Furthermore, the language design should be unambiguous to remove all doubt about precisely what operations will be performed and what the result should be. Unfortunately, this is not always the case with some complex languages such as Algol-68 or with loosely defined languages such as Fortran; programs that are written in these languages may exhibit differences in their behaviour when they are executed on different computer systems if the language rules are given different interpretations by the systems. The differences may arise from either a lack of precision in the language definition or from weak rules for its implementation which allow some features to be optional or which leave some aspects to be implementation-dependant.

1.2.4.1. Guarded commands and non-deterministic programs

The program constructs introduced in the previous section are deterministic: the result of the execution of a program statement is uniquely determined by the state of the program variables immediately before its execution. In many ways this simplifies the programming and testing of programs, especially where informal methods are employed.

Dijkstra (1975) has argued that the design and implementation of programs may be better expressed in a non-deterministic manner. He introduced the concept of the *<guarded_command>*. A *<guarded_command>* consists of a boolean expression, the *<guard>*, followed by a series of program statements, the *<guarded_list>*. The *<guarded_list>* is eligible for execution only when its *<guard>* evaluates to *true*. For example,

$$x > y \rightarrow max := x$$

is a *<guarded_command>* in which the assignment becomes eligible if x is greater than y. Sets of *<guarded_command>*s may be assembled into two forms of constructs which may be used as program statements, the *<alternative_construct>* and the *<repetitive_construct>*. The component commands are delineated by the special symbol □. The order in which the *<guarded_command>*s appear is purely arbitrary and does not imply any sequencing or priority between them.

The *<alternative_construct>* is delineated by the symbols **if** and **fi**. For example,

if
$$x >= y \rightarrow max := x$$
□
$$y >= x \rightarrow max := y$$
fi

is a statement with two alternatives. When control reaches the statement all the guards are evaluated to determine which *<guarded_list>*s are eligible. One eligible *<guarded_list>* is then selected in a non-deterministic manner and is executed; control then proceeds to the next program statement. If no guards evaluate to *true*, the program aborts. The example given above will set the value of *max* to the greater of *x* or *y*. If both variables have the same value, both assignments are eligible and an arbitrary choice will be made by the implementation.

The *<repetitive_construct>* is delineated by the symbols **do** and **od**. The guards are repeatedly evaluated and an eligible *<guarded_list>* is executed. Control passes to the next program statement only when no guards evaluate to *true*. The statement:-

do

        q1 > q2 →
                temp := q1;
                q1 := q2;
                q2 := temp

   ◻   *q2 > q3* →
                temp := q2;
                q2 := q3;
                q3 := temp

   ◻   *q3 > q4* →
                temp := q3;
                q3 := q4;
                q4 := temp

od

will not terminate until the values of the four variables are sorted into ascending order, i.e. $q1 <= q2 <= q3 <= q4$. The sequence in which the pairs of values are swapped is not defined and could differ for various executions of the program.

An advantage of guarded commands is that the programmer is not required to specify superfluous detail concerning how a program is to be executed. Furthermore, guarded commands are particularly useful for coping with inherent non-determinism of concurrent programs. Constructs of this form are found in several languages discussed in later chapters.

1.2.5. Procedures, functions and parameters

The basic statements of the previous section are analogues to simple data types and variables. Procedures and functions correspond to structured data types, since they collect together sequences of related statements. An alternative view is to regard them as small programs. In most languages procedures and functions are very similar in structure and usage. The following paragraphs will outline Pascal procedures; they are followed by a brief summary of the differences exhibited by functions.

There are two aspects to using procedures, their declaration and their use. The first aspect is the formal procedure definition which gives the procedure a name, declares the variables private to the procedure, and defines the program code or 'procedure body'. The procedure may then be used in a program by using the procedure name as a statement. When control reaches the statement, the procedure is 'called'; in effect a new block is entered, the declaration of local variables is elaborated and the procedure body is executed. The following simple example would result in 'Hello' being written five times:-

```
        procedure hello;
        begin
                writeln ("Hello")
        end;                      {procedure declared}

begin
        for i := 1 to 5 do
                hello             {procedure called}
end.
```

The procedure definition given above is of limited use since it always performs exactly the same operations. Most languages provide a parametrisation mechanism which allows procedures to be defined in a more general manner. The precise operations to be performed are determined when the procedure is called at which point the actual values to be used in place of the formal parameters are specified.

Pascal usually provides two parametrisation mechanisms, both provide flexibility in the use of variables. The heading of a procedure definition may include a list of the names of its parameters and the parameters' types. This list specifies the 'formal parameters'. The names of the formal parameters may then be used within the definition of the procedure body as if they were declared as local variables within the procedure.

When the procedure is called, a list of actual parameters must be given which are then used during that particular execution of the procedure. The values specified in the list of 'actual parameters' are used in place of the formal parameters in the corresponding position in the formal parameter list. In Pascal, the compiler may check that the correct number of actual parameters are supplied, and that their types are compatible with the types of the formal parameters. Some language implementations provide less stringent checks at the procedure's interface and require the programmer to enforce the correspondence between actual and formal parameters; this is particularly true of languages such as C and Fortran which allow the separate compilation of parts of the program. However, more recent languages, such as Modula-2 and Ada, do enforce stringent checks between the parts of a program that are compiled separately.

The first of Pascal's two parametrisation mechanisms is the use of 'value' parameters. Value parameters allow initial values to be provided for formal parameters. The actual parameter is used solely to specify an initial value for the corresponding formal parameter. Therefore any expression, including simply a variable name, may be specified as the actual parameter, provided that it delivers a value of the correct type. The following example demonstrates the use of a value parameter and results in the numbers 1 to 5 being written as the output of the program:-

```
procedure writeno (j : integer);
begin
          writeln (j)        {write value of parameter}
end;


begin
     for i := 1 to 5 do
          writeno (i)        {call procedure with different values}
end.
```

In this example the variable *j* acts just like any local variable except that it is initialised before the procedure is executed. There is no continuing relationship between the formal parameter and any variable used to pass the initial value. The parameter supplied when the procedure is called need not be a variable; any expression delivering a result of the correct type may be used. Using the procedure definition in the above example,

   writeno (5 + 4);

is perfectly acceptable.

The above examples have made use of the 'standard procedure' *writeln* which results in data being written to the output. The idea of 'standard procedures' is common to many languages. They are supplied by the language implementation to provide useful operations, such as input, output and frequently used functions (e.g. trigonometric functions), and do not need to be declared by the user. Some standard procedures, such as *writeln* allow more flexibility in the provision of actual parameters than user-defined procedures enjoy. For example, *writeln* will accept any number of parameters, and the type of each parameter may be one of a range of acceptable types. *writeln* adapts its operation to accommodate its actual parameters.

The second of Pascal's parametrisation mechanisms allows procedures to return results to the calling program by updating variables as well as passing initial values to the procedure. The actual parameters must therefore identify variables of the correct type which are updated by the procedure. It is not possible, therefore, to use an expression for the actual parameter. Parameters of this form are called 'variable' or 'reference' parameters and are prefixed by the reserved word **var** in Pascal. For example, the following procedure doubles the value supplied by the first parameter and returns the result by updating the value of the variable supplied as the second parameter.

```
            procedure double (in : integer; var out : integer);
            begin
                    out := in + in
            end;


    begin
            double (5,j)
    end.
```

The effect of the above program is that the value of j will be set to 10. In practice variable parameters are often implemented by supplying the called procedure with a reference to the actual parameter, i.e. by passing the address of the variable to be used. All operations that are performed on the formal parameter in the body of the procedure are implemented indirectly on the variable supplied as the actual parameter. An alternative implementation is to initialise a local variable, as with value parameters; the procedure is then executed using the local variable and the result is copied back to the actual parameter on procedure exit.

Functions differ from procedures in that they return a value as a result of their execution. They are used, therefore, as expressions and not as statements. Function definitions differ from procedure definitions in three minor ways: they are introduced by the reserved word **function** rather than **procedure**; the type of result delivered by the function is specified in its heading; and the body contains a statement assigning the result of the function's execution to the function's name. Functions are called in the same way as procedures and use the same parameter mechanisms. The following example implements the previous example by means of a function.

```
            function double (in : integer) : integer;
            begin
                    double:= in + in
            end;


    begin
            j := double (5)
    end.
```

Rules concerning the declaration of procedures tend to reflect those governing the declaration of variables. The scope rules defining the parts of a program from which they may be accessed reflect, in a similar manner, the access constraints on variables. Thus some languages such as Fortran or C only provide a 'flat' structure consisting of a series of procedure definitions followed by the main body of the program which calls them. Pascal and derived languages allow for the nesting of procedure definitions so that procedures may contain private sub-procedures that are only accessible in the immediately enclosing and in the enclosed procedure definitions.

```
procedure outer;
var      {declare variables local to outer}
         a, b : integer;

         procedure level1;
         var      {declare variables local to level1}
                  c, d : integer;

                  procedure level2;
                  var      {declare variables local to level2}
                           e, f : integer;

                  begin
                           e := 5 + 4
                  end; {of level2}

         begin
                  ...
         end; {of level1}

begin
         ...
end; {outer}
```

Fig. 1.3 - A nested program.

An example of a nested program structure is given in Fig. 1.3. Each procedure may declare its own local variables which may be accessed in its main body or from the body of any of its local procedures. Thus *outer's* variables are accessible to all three procedures but *level2's* are only accessible from within the procedure. Note that every time a procedure is called a new set of its own local variables are created, but not those of its sub-procedures.

A procedure may call any global procedures that are within its scope; thus *level2* may call *level1*, *outer*, and any enclosing procedures. A procedure may also call any of its direct sub-procedures, but not nested ones. Thus *outer* may call *level1* but not *level2*. A procedure may also call itself, allowing recursive operations to be defined. There is no theoretical limit to the mutual calling of procedures; *level1* may use *level2* and vice-versa, so several instances of a procedure may exist at one time. This is analogous to using a type definition to define several similar variables. Each time a procedure is called, a new set of its local variables are generated and operated upon. These are independent of any other variables generated by other calls to the same procedure. The way in which this may be implemented is examined in the next section.

1.2.6. Memory allocation

The details of the representation of a program in a computer's memory is dependent on many details of the underlying hardware, on the environment provided by the operating system software, and on how the language implementor chooses to work within these limitations. However, most implementations of a block-structured language are based around the same techniques; once the principles are understood detailed implementations are easily assimilated.

Procedures and blocks may be entered any number of times during program execution, and the limit is unknown during compilation. The compiler must therefore generate 're-entrant' code which is reusable and executed each time a procedure is called. Each time a procedure is entered, a different memory area must be reserved for the local variables. Since several calls to the same procedure may be active simultaneously, the same code must be able to reference, safely and securely, the many different memory areas. The particular memory area to be used is determined dynamically, and depends on the context in which the procedure is executed. For this to work, the code must always be the same, and so must not modify itself. Nor may it contain any absolute addresses of program data variables since the absolute addresses are only allocated on a procedure's execution.

Block-structured languages restrict the lifetime of data variables to that of their enclosing block. This means that memory resources for data variables may be allocated as they are needed on entry to a procedure or block and then deallocated on exit. Memory allocation is usually implemented using a 'stack' mechanism which corresponds to the discipline of procedure entry and exit. A contiguous area of memory is designated as the stack area and it is used to represent all the program variables. Initially all the area is free for use and one end is designated the start or top of the stack. As procedures or blocks are entered, successive suitable sized segments, known as 'stack frames', are allocated from the free area at the current top of the stack. On procedure exit these segments are returned to the free area. In this way the memory is allocated only when it is actually in use and it may be re-used later by other procedures. The position of the top of the stack is usually indicated by a machine register designated the 'stack pointer' or 'sp'. Stacks and their operation are covered in more detail in appendix A.

When the memory area is allocated for a block, a pointer to the start of the area is stored in a register. The individual variables within the segment are then accessed using an offset from this base address. In this way the instructions generated only contain the offsets of the variables within the segment, which may be determined on compilation; the allocation and selection of the actual addresses is delayed until the program's execution.

At most points in a program several sets of variables of the enclosing blocks are potentially accessible. These are also accessed as offsets in their segments and some mechanism must be provided to locate the bottoms of the segments. Fig. 1.4 illustrates the allocation of procedure variables on a stack. Some computers have hardware registers for this, but most smaller ones have to do it in software either by using a reserved memory area or by including references in each segment to link them together.

The final use of the stack is to store temporary results during expression evaluation. To do this the compiler usually re-orders expressions from a high-level language into a 'reverse polish notation'. In this form operands are evaluated and placed on the stack before the operator is called. On evaluation the operands are removed and replaced by the result. For example, the expression:-

$$5 + 4$$

would translate into a program

put 5 on stack
put 4 on stack
add

leaving the result, 9, on top of the stack. This notation follows the stack discipline and allows the evaluation of arbitrarily complex expressions including the integrated evaluation of user-defined functions.

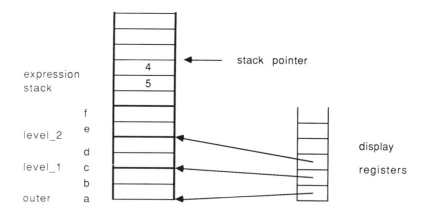

Fig. 1.4 - Allocation of procedure variables.

1.2.7. Dynamic allocation

The previous discussion has concentrated on the allocation of variables within procedures. These 'static' variables are intimately connected to the procedures in which they are declared, and may only be created on procedure or block entry and disappear on exit. Although adequate for most purposes, they are unsatisfactory for handling systems in which an unknown number of events might take place and need to be recorded. Using static variables, it is necessary to declare a large array of variables hoping that it will be adequate. The disadvantages of this scheme lie in its inflexibility and in that it wastes memory if only few instances occur.

An alternative approach is via 'dynamic allocation' which allows new variables to be created independently of the static policy of the block structure. Dynamic variables are not intimately associated with particular procedures and therefore cannot be allocated space on the stack. Instead they require an independent allocation strategy. The area reserved for their allocation is called the 'heap', since it may be used in a random manner. Since dynamic variables cannot be generated by a declaration they cannot be given individual identifiers by which they can be referenced in the program text. Instead they are generated and referenced indirectly through pointer variables. The standard procedure *new* in Pascal takes any form of pointer variable as a parameter and sets it to reference a new object of the appropriate form. The memory required for the object is allocated from the heap. By generating new record variables which themselves contain pointer variables, dynamic data structures of interlinked objects may be created. Programming with these dynamic techniques is covered in more detail in Appendix A.

Four policies may be adopted for the controlled disposal of dynamic variables. The first is 'garbage collection'. This is the most simple to use for the programmer and the most complex to implement. The burden of reclaiming storage for variables that are no longer required is placed on the language implementation software. Reassigning values to pointer variables may cause the objects that they previously referenced to be inaccessible to the program, in which case the memory may be safely reclaimed and re-used. Periodically the underlying software system examines all the dynamic variables and reclaims those that are inaccessible to the user's program. This can be a very complex and expensive process.

A second policy is sometimes adopted which requires the user to free a variable explicitly using a standard procedure such as *dispose*. In this scheme inaccessible objects are not reclaimed and the user risks exhausting the available memory if objects are simply discarded without being 'disposed'.

Disposing of large numbers of objects can be quite difficult and time consuming, especially if they form a complex data structure. In some application programs, such as compilers, the allocation and disposal of dynamic variables may follow a stack-like discipline. Some dynamic allocation schemes allocate space from the heap in a stack-like manner. This allows the programmer in effect to discard all the variables allocated after a particular point in the program's execution by repositioning the heap's stack pointer.

The final approach to reclamation is to ignore it completely, and to hope the user does not request too much memory, a policy which may be reasonable in machines with very large virtual memories.

1.2.8. Summary of sequential programs

High-level languages have evolved to discipline the use of computers, to enhance their usability and to improve the reliability of software. To this end the procedural languages have evolved simple control statements to formalise algorithms, data-typing to control the access to variables, and advanced data structures to aid structured program design.

During execution, the program consists of three components:-

(1)   A memory area reserved for the program variables used as the program stack, and possibly another heap area for dynamic variables.

(2)   The code of a series of procedure definitions. These are re-entrant and reusable and do not refer to any absolute memory locations.

(3)   The values established in the hardware registers of the machine.

Many of the registers are used to indicate significant memory addresses in the data area, such as the top of the stack or the bases of stack frames. It is these registers which provide the 'context' in which the machine instructions are interpreted. They provide the environment in which the conceptual addresses contained in the program code are transformed into real machine addresses. Changing the context registers allows the same procedure definition to be repeatedly used throughout a program.

1.3. PROGRAMS AND PROCESSES

Programs are like procedure definitions: they define a sequence of operations but do not do anything until they are actually executed. For a program to be executed, memory resources have to be allocated for its use and the addresses of these memory areas must be loaded into the hardware registers. The execution of a sequential program is often referred to as a 'process' in operating systems terminology. Unfortunately there are a number of definitions or meanings for the term, but this one is adequate in this context. The term 'task' is often used with a similar meaning. Neither term has an adequate accepted definition. The same program may be executed a number of times, giving a series of processes. Assuming that the entire program is written using re-entrant coding techniques, different invocations of the program could be initialised to be executed using different memory areas by loading different values into the machine's registers. This is analogous to the repeated calls to a procedure. Although the processes would be executed using different memory addresses for variables, the results produced by each process should be the same.

If the machine consisted of a single memory area, but had a number of hardware processors each with their own complete set of registers, it would be possible to initialise each processor's registers so that they each executed programs using different memory areas for their variables. This machine would be able to implement a number of processes simultaneously; some could be executing the same program, using the same code definition; others could implement different programs. Provided that the various processors' registers are initialised appropriately so that all the program data areas are disjoint, each process should be unaware of the concurrent execution of the other processes.

The ability to run a number of software processes concurrently on the same machine is useful when they each interface to separate external processes. Unfortunately, providing separate registers and processor hardware for each process can be expensive, and if some of them are idle at times it is not very cost-effective. These problems are overcome by sequentially sharing the processor hardware between the software processes. The sharing is achieved in stages:

(1)   The values of the registers are set to those of one process and the process begins to be executed using the program code and data areas defined by the contents of the registers.

(2)   At some stage the processor ceases to perform the operations of that process, stores the contents of all the registers, loads a new address context and begins to execute a different process.

(3)   The processor continuously implements a process for some time before changing to another process. Eventually the processor retrieves the context that it saved when it stopped executing the first process. The context is reloaded into its registers and the execution of the process is resumed from the point at which it had ceased.

The processor continues this manner; loading a process and executing it for a while before switching to another process. In this way all the processes appear to proceed in their execution, but at a slower rate than they could achieve if each process were given a dedicated processor.

Processor multiplexing is a very common technique; apart from very primitive machines most processors provide some degree of hardware support for changing contexts.

1.4. PROCESS SCHEDULING

Multiplexing the processor to produce multiple processes may be usefully employed in several parts of a software system.

(1)   It is usually employed at the core of any system's software as a technique for handling peripheral devices using the hardware interrupt mechanism. This is covered in more detail in Chapter 7. Only very primitive microprocessors do not support this basic level of

multiplexing.

(2)   Many operating systems provide support for generating and managing multiple processes. In the case of large multi-user time-sharing systems, the emphasis is on providing a service for independent users and preventing their mutual interference. Operating systems oriented to real-time control tend to provide for greater interaction between processes. In contrast, some micro-computer based operating systems do not provide support for multiple user processes.

(3)   Multiple-processes may be defined in a single program in a concurrent programming language. The processes may then be implemented in one of two ways, depending on the facilities provided by the underlying operating system.

Given suitable facilities, it may be possible for each of the processes defined in the program to be implemented by a separate operating system process. In this case all of the context saving and swapping is handled by the underlying operating system routines. However, the operating system may not provide the user with multiple processes, or may not provide appropriate mechanisms for the processes to co-operate with each other. In such cases, processor multiplexing must be provided by the software which implements the language. Thus a process defined in a concurrent program running on a multi-user operating system may undergo two levels of multiplexing. These techniques are illustrated in Fig. 1.5.

The management of multiple processes requires that details of the status of each process is stored as well as its context. This is stored in a record structure called a 'process-descriptor'. The successful operation of multiple processes involves some sophistication in the algorithms used to determine the sequence in which processes are to be executed and when they are to be suspended. This is referred to as 'scheduling'. In order to implement scheduling the process-descriptors are usually maintained in a number of lists depending on their status. These are usually implemented as a number of linked lists using a pointer field in the process-descriptor (see Appendix A for details of list manipulation algorithms).

Any halted processes which could be immediately resumed are kept in the 'ready queue'. When the processor is available to service a new process, the process-descriptor is removed from the head of the ready queue and the context loaded into the processor's registers. Some operating systems allow the programmer to indicate the relative importance of processes by defining their 'priority'. This is usually defined by some integer value and is stored in the process-descriptor. The ready queue is then either maintained as a sorted list with the highest priority processes at the front, or it may be implemented as a series of lists of different priorities. Conventions vary between systems: some systems regard low numbers as the highest priority with 0 or 1 as the most important. Other systems take high numbers as higher priority with 0 indicating the lowest priority.

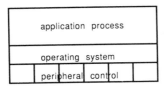

i) Multiple processes within o/s only

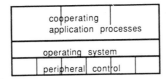

ii) Time Sharing System.

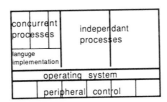

iii) Real-time System

iv) Concurrent Program on Time-shared System.

Fig. 1.5 - Implementations of Processes.

A variety of events may cause a process to become deallocated. Processes are often given a 'time-slice' which is the maximum continuous period for which they can remain allocated. Once the time-slice has expired a process will be deallocated and its descriptor inserted at a suitable point in the ready queue. Time-slicing ensures that no one process can monopolise the processor. The overall performance of the system can be manipulated by adjusting the time-slices and the priorities of the component processes.

A process may voluntarily suspend its operation. For example, some processes are required to run only periodically to monitor some occurrence. This is facilitated by a 'delay' operation which allows the process to request its deallocation and reallocation at some particular time in the future. This is usually implemented by keeping a queue of delayed processes which is sorted into the order of their resumption with their restart time stored in the process-descriptor. The head of the queue may be examined periodically and when its restart time is reached the process is allocated or its process-descriptor is promoted to the ready queue.

Finally, a process may be deallocated if it is delayed waiting for some operation to be performed by another process. It may be explicitly waiting for a message from another processor or for input from a peripheral device. Alternatively, it may be waiting to gain access to a shared resource that is currently being accessed by another process. All these cases can be handled by some similar 'event' mechanism. The underlying system maintains the process-descriptors of all delayed processes in either one queue or a series of queues, awaiting the occurrence of a significant event. When the executing process wishes to communicate with another process or to release some shared resource, it requests the underlying system to perform the action on its behalf. The system then determines whether this event is being awaited by another process, and if so, the waiting process is promoted to the ready queue. The details of these mechanisms will be examined in greater detail in later chapters.

1.5. SUMMARY AND FURTHER READING

This chapter has examined some aspects of the design and implementation of sequential programming languages. Rather than simply detailing the features present in any particular language it has attempted to show why certain common features are found in many languages. This involves understanding not only how the features are used, but also how they may be implemented. Language designs are examined further in the book by Young (1982). Compiler design and its interrelationship with hardware is covered by Gries (1971), and Aho and Ullman (1978). An enlightening study of the overall process of language design and implementation is proved by Pemberton and Daniels' (1982) book on P4 Pascal.

Language design has also influenced the design of computer architecture. Many machines have incorporated features, such as hardware stacks, to aid language implementors. The Burroughs computers have perhaps gone furthest towards providing hardware support of block structured languages (Organick, 1973). On a smaller scale the DEC PDP11 family provide many useful features including numerous sophisticated addressing modes to aid the programming of stack operations and the use of relative addressing (Eckhouse, 1979). The two main families of microprocessor architectures include features that are intended to aid the implementation of complex systems; however, the two designs emphasise the support of different aspects of software implementation. The Motorola 68000 family (King, 1983) provides an extensive and easily manipulated memory address space, whereas the Intel 80286 family (Intel, 1985) is more complex to program but provides extensive hardware support for multiple processes and context switching.

The introduction to sequential program design, to its implementation and to multiple processes that is provided by this chapter should provide much of the necessary basis for understanding the implementation principles of concurrent programming languages; however, it does not provide the complete picture. The concurrent programming techniques and their implementations require the additional concepts of interprocess cooperation and coordination. Consequently, the material presented so far is inadequate to explain fully the implementation of multiple processes and their scheduling. An adequate explanation also requires the consideration of these additional concepts, which are the subject of the next chapter.

2

Process Coordination

2.1. INTRODUCTION

The previous chapter introduced the concept of a process by describing it as
the execution of a program. This is an over-simplification, since some programs define a number of processes which may be executed concurrently.

A variety of techniques have been used to define potential concurrency.
Some work has been done towards the automatic introduction of multiple
processes by compilers. This approach is quite successful in producing
optimised code for special array processors but it is not in general use.

Since identifying potential concurrency can be quite complex, most
languages require the programmer to specify which parts of a program are
suitable for concurrent execution. Algol-68 allows the programmer to identify series of statements with the potential for concurrent execution by
prefixing them with the symbol **par**; for example, the statement:-

> **par begin**
> > *a := 1,*
> > *b := 2,*
> > *c := 3*
> **end;**

signifies that the three assignments may be performed concurrently. All three
assignments must be completed before the parallel statement completes and
control passes to the next program statement.

In practice, the relatively high costs of process creation and resynchronisation mean that a program sequence must be quite large before the generation of a separate process is worthwhile. For this reason alternative notations are sometimes employed.

A common technique is to provide that standard procedures *fork* and *join* to indicate sections of the program which may be executed in parallel. *Fork* takes a procedure name as its parameter and causes it to be executed as a separate process; there may also be facilities to pass parameters to the new process. The new process is said to be a 'child' or 'daughter' process of the 'parent'.

Process creation is performed by the underlying support mechanisms which allocate the child a unique name or 'process-id'. This process-id is usually returned to the parent for later use. The two processes then proceed independently; eventually the child process may complete its execution and terminate.

The parent process may use the *join* operation to synchronise its execution with the termination of one of its child processes; the process-id of the child must be supplied as a parameter to *join*. If the child has terminated before the parent calls the *join* operation the parent may continue immediately; otherwise the parent must wait for the child to terminate. Any results that may have been delivered by the execution of the child process may be passed back to the parent process at this point.

The following example illustrates how *fork* and *join* might be used. The variable *p* is assumed to be of type 'process-id' and that the *fork* and *join* functions have flexible parameter types (like *writeln* in Pascal).†

```
var
     p        : process-id;
     result   : integer;

     function square (i : integer): integer;
     begin
             square := i * i
     end;

begin
     p := fork (square, 2);              {create child}
     ...
     <concurrent computations>
     ...
     result := join (p);                 {retrieve result}
end.
```

---

† The examples in this book will, whenever possible, follow the convention of including program comments in curly brackets {}. Angle brackets, <>, will be used to indicate pseudocode, which is used to summarise program code where the detail is irrelevant to the discussion.

Facilities of this form are provided in the language Mesa (Lampson 1980). Some languages do not provide the resynchronisation of parent and child processes; such independent children are said to be 'detached'.

The two processes in the above example differ significantly from those of Chapter 1 since their execution is co-ordinated: they are co-operating towards the common goal of the program. This example demonstrates the two aspects of coordination: communication and synchronisation.

Communication
> is the transfer of data values from one process to another.

Synchronization
> involves the transmission of status information concerning the state of a process or the system.

A number of process coordination methodologies have been proposed or implemented and representative examples of these methodologies are examined in detail in Part II of this book. Their differences depend on the extent to which process communication and synchronisation is made explicit or implicit by the facilities provided.

The above example involves the explicit communication of data between the two processes as parameters and results, and the explicit synchronisation of the processes at the creation and termination of the child process. Other methodologies are more asynchronous and the information being exchanged may either be stored in a buffer by underlying support software, or simply discarded. The sender of the information does not know if, or when, it is received by the target process. Neither does the receiver know when the information was sent nor what the other process has done since the information was dispatched.

Alternatively, the methodology may not provide any explicit synchronisation mechanism, so processes must deduce the status of other processes indirectly from the values of common data variables.

In practice both synchronous and asynchronous coordination of processes is often required. In such cases it is necessary for the programmer to implement an alternative mechanism using the primitive operations supplied with the language. Part II of the book gives some examples of these techniques.

2.2. EXAMPLES OF CONCURRENT PROCESSES

The use of multiple processes is illustrated by the two following examples which will be used throughout the book to illustrate the various implementation techniques.

The first example is an instrument which is required to sample its input data at some constant and frequent rate. The individual data values are not required for output; only the mean values and standard deviations for given periods are needed. These values are collected and stored periodically on some non volatile medium, or are transmitted to a supervisory computer. The system may be simply implemented using three asynchronous processes to perform the three functions of sampling, data manipulation and data storage as shown in Fig. 2.1. This organisation is more suitable for the problem than a monolithic program, since the three processes work on different time-scales: whilst the sampling process must proceed at a fixed regular interval, the storage or transmission process may take an unpredictable time because of external factors such as disk head positioning delays or communication line errors. In practice, timing constraints may necessitate the use of multiple hardware processors even in a system as simple as this.

Both aspects of process coordination are illustrated by this example. The various processes communicate to pass on data as it is processed. The logger's input process must be explicitly synchronised with some external hardware clock device so that it may sample its input at fixed intervals. Since each of the other processes may proceed only after receiving adequate input data they too are synchronised to some degree. The degree of synchronisation is dependent on the method and implementation of the communication mechanism between the processes. For instance, a process may either forward every item of data as it becomes available, or it may accumulate and forward blocks of data to give a more loosely coupled program.

The second example will consider a control system for a carpark with a number of entrances and exits which are controlled by automatic barriers. The overall purpose of the system is to control the flow of vehicles into the carpark so that there are always a parking space available for each vehicle that enters.

This is a typical resource-allocation problem where the processes which control the several entrances compete for parking spaces for their waiting

Fig. 2.1 - Implementation of the data-logger.

cars. For this problem some mechanisms must be devised so that an arbitrary number of processes agree on the residual number of cars in the park at any time, allowing for the fact that cars are constantly entering and leaving by the several exits.

The problem differs significantly from the data-logger problem in a number of ways. Whereas the logger involved coordination between pairs of processes, the carpark essentially involves the mutual coordination of many processes. The three processes of the logger were all cooperating towards a common end of collecting and storing the data, and its performance is judged solely on how well this goal is achieved.

The carpark processes, however, are in 'competition' with each other when there are more customers than spaces. The system is judged not only on its ability to admit the correct number of cars, but also on the fairness and flexibility of the policy used to determine when to admit a car. For instance, the program would probably be considered unsatisfactory if one entrance continually admits cars while vehicles are kept waiting elsewhere.

Another difference is that the logger involves some tight synchronisation within stringent timing constraints, whilst the carpark processes are essentially asynchronous, and the overall operation of the system is determined by the arbitrary behaviour of the customers.

The two systems serve to illustrate the difference between 'real-time' and 'online' systems. Real-time systems must respond to the external environment within some critical time. Failure to respond within this limit results in loss of incoming data or loss of control of some external system. Whilst the logger is a trivial real-time system, air-traffic control systems are more demanding.

Online systems also interact with the external environment but the rate of interaction is under the control of the computer. The carpark is a good example in this respect, since the automatic barriers control the rate at which cars enter and leave. Normally the cars will be flexible in the amount of time they will wait for the system to respond to their presence. If the system response becomes so slow that cars do not wait but go elsewhere the system does not actually lose control or data, only customers.

The control of a user's terminal is also an online operation since the user will adapt his behaviour to match the computer's performance. This flexibility in the overall functioning of the whole system means that online programs generally are much easier to design than their real-time counterparts.

The remaining sections of this chapter will examine the most basic mechanisms used for process interaction. These methods illustrate the intricacy of the problems to be encountered, and the difficulty of proving the correctness of such programs even at an informal level. After this discussion the need for the higher level abstraction mechanisms, introduced in Part II of the book, should become more apparent.

The next section examines the use of variables shared by a pair of processes; this example demonstrates most of the problems to be encountered with multi-processed systems consisting of either a multiplexed single processor or a real multiprocessor with memory that may be shared by the several processors.

The first successful attempt to provide a formal solution to these problems proposed the introduction of a special type of variable called the semaphore, with special operations defined for its use. These are discussed in the following section. The semaphore is adequate for solving most, if not all, problems of process coordination, but it is a very low-level tool and difficult to use. The chapter ends with a summary of the problems to be solved by any multi-processed programming methodology.

2.3. ACCESSING SHARED VARIABLES

The simplest implementation of coordination between the processes of a concurrent program is to allow some data variables to be accessed by more than one process. Unfortunately, this simple approach can lead to program errors when two processes simultaneously access the same set of variables. For instance the carpark controller might maintain a commonly accessible variable, *spaces*, recording the number of spaces available. This is updated by each gate-controlling process whenever a car enters or leaves. Thus the departure of a car would cause one of the processes to execute the statement:-

   spaces := spaces + 1

This statement results in the execution of at least three basic operations.

(1)   The value of *spaces* is copied into a working register or onto the expression stack.

(2)   The value 1 is added to it.

(3)   The result is stored back into *spaces*.

This is quite satisfactory when there is only one process, but problems may arise when two processes attempt the update simultaneously. Both will read the same initial value of *spaces*, add one to it, and then both will store the same value with the result that one update is effectively lost. The problems arise from the interleaving of the machine level operations of the processes during the execution of a logical operation. These sorts of errors are extremely difficult to detect by program testing since they depend on the precise interaction and timing of two independent processes. These 'lurking bugs' may exist for years within software before they exhibit themselves. Rather than trying to prove the absence of such faults by testing, designs must be structured so that they cannot arise. Program segments which access common variables are often referred to as 'critical regions', and a programmer must be careful to identify all the critical regions of a program.

The programmer must prevent separate processes from simultaneously executing critical regions which contain common variables. In a few special cases this may be done by implementing the critical region by a single indivisible processor instruction. For instance, many processors have an 'increment store' instruction which adds 1 to the contents of a memory location; this could be suitable for updating *spaces*. However this is a special case; the problem of enforcing longer critical regions is bound to arise when updating complex data structures which involve a number of variables, such as tables or lists. In these cases the programmer must implement software protocols to ensure the integrity of the data structures. This may be done by using the basic indivisible operations to create 'locks' to limit the access to the larger structures. A policy of 'mutual exclusion' of processes is usually adopted, whereby a process is granted access to a structure to the exclusion of all other processes.

The case of a car wishing to enter the carpark gives an example of a longer critical region. The process must first determine if there is a free space before allocating it to the waiting car, i.e.

```
if spaces > 0 then
        begin
                spaces := spaces - 1;
                <admit_customer>
        end
else
        <indicate_delay>
```

This test and conditional decrement operation is unlikely to be implemented as a single instruction in a general purpose computer; even if it is provided, some other sequence of operations that are required probably will not be implemented. Mutual exclusion during update of *spaces* will have to be provided by some locking mechanism, which is invoked before the variable is accessed and released on completion of the update, i.e.

```
lock;                           {gain exclusive access}
if spaces > 0 then
        begin
                spaces := spaces - 1;
                <admit_customer>
        end
else
        <indicate_delay>;
unlock;                         {release exclusive access}
```

It is important that every program segment that manipulates *spaces* is bracketed by a pair of calls to *lock* and *unlock*. The departure of a car therefore must also be coded as:

```
lock;
spaces := spaces + 1;
unlock;
```

One implication of the mutual exclusion policy is that some processes may be delayed waiting for access to variables that are locked by another process. To minimise the general disruption of the functioning of the entire system, it is desirable to lock data items for the minimum time possible, and not to enforce exclusion during the execution of statements which do not manipulate common variables. For example, the entry of a car may be better encoded using a local boolean variable to record the result of accessing the shared data, i.e.

```
lock;                    {gain exclusive access}
if spaces > 0 then
        begin
                spaces := spaces - 1;
                ok := true
        end
else
        ok := false;
unlock;                  {release exclusive access}

if ok then
        <admit_customer>
else
        <indicate_delay>
```

This avoids delaying all other processes while the waiting car enters, since this is an operation which takes a long time compared to the execution of other parts of the program.

Similar considerations of efficiency mean that it may be desirable to implement a number of locks which control access to separate sections of the shared data. In this way several processes may proceed concurrently provided that they are accessing disjoint sets of shared variables.

2.3.1. Implementing locks using shared variables

This section will develop a lock protocol that provides mutual exclusion between two processes without the aid of sophisticated indivisible operations. Implementing the lock by simply setting or testing the value of a common variable has already been seen to be inappropriate because of possible interleaving of its access. A number of refinements will be developed which serve to illustrate the problems that may be encountered when implementing concurrent systems.

The interleaving problem may be overcome by introducing two variables (sometimes called flags), one for each process. Both processes may read

the values of both variables, but the authority to update each variable is restricted to one process per variable. This avoids the problem of two processes
simultaneously updating the same variable. The basis of this lock protocol is
that a process will proceed if, and only if, it has set its own flag and the other
process does not have its flag set. The lock may be implemented by the two
procedures:-

```
procedure lock (var my_flag, his_flag : boolean);
begin
        my_flag := true; {indicate intention to claim lock}
        while his_flag do;          {repeatedly test and wait for}
                                    {other process if necessary};
end;


procedure unlock (var my_flag : boolean);
begin
        my_flag := false {release claim on critical region}
end;
```

The procedure parameters are passed by reference to ensure that actual global
variables, and not local copies, are set or tested every time. The procedures
would both be called by both processes, but the order in which the parameters
are supplied provides the interchange of function of the variables. The following program sample indicates their use:-

```
var flag_1, flag_2 : boolean := false; {both flags initialised to false}

process_1:
begin
        ...
        lock (flag_1, flag_2);

        <access protected data>

        unlock (flag_1);
        ...
end;

process_2:
begin
        ...
        lock (flag_2, flag_1);

        <access protected data>

        unlock (flag_2);
        ...
end;
```

Notice the symmetry of the program: both processes are equal in status. Either process may attempt to claim the lock and may set its own flag, which initially is set to *false*. The process then tests the value of the other process' flag resulting in one of two cases.

(1)   The most likely case is that the other process is not currently accessing the data. In this case its flag will be false and the process may safely proceed to access the data. To release the lock when it has completed, it may simply reset its own flag to *false*.

(2)   The other case may arise when the other process has already claimed the lock and is already accessing the shared data. In this case the entering process must repeatedly test the other flag until the other process unlocks the data by resetting its flag. This sequence of operation of the two processes is shown below:-

Process_1	*Process_2*
...	...
set own flag	...
test other flag - false	...
{lock now set}	...
...	*set own flag*
<access shared data>	*test other flag - true*
...	*test other flag - true*
...	*test other flag - true*
reset own flag	*test other flag - false*
...	*{lock now set}*
...	...
...	*<access shared data>*
...	*reset own flag*
...	*{lock now clear}*
...	...
...	...

The protocol is symmetrical; whichever process attempts to set the lock first is allowed to proceed and the second process will wait for it to complete its critical section in the event of a clash. It does of course rely on both processes being well-behaved. Both processes must wait for the other process if necessary, and both processes must release the lock at some stage.

However, there is a major flaw in the protocol. This arises if both processes attempt to claim the lock simultaneously. Each process may set its own flag and then test the other flag giving a *true* result. Both processes will assume that the other process is already accessing the shared data and will repeatedly test the other flag waiting for the other to complete its access and unlock the data. The sequence is shown below:-

```
Process_1                          Process_2
...                                ...
set own flag                       set own flag
test other flag - true             test other flag -  true
test other flag - true             test other flag -  true
test other flag - true             test other flag -  true
etc
```

Both processes will be delayed indefinitely, each waiting for the other to perform some action before it may proceed. Such situations are called 'deadlock'.

2.3.2. Revised locking scheme

The problem with the previous protocol is that a process resets its own flag only after it has completed accessing the shared data. A possible solution to the deadlock problem is to require that a process resets its own flag during the locking procedure if it finds the other process' flag already set. This could be programmed as:-

```
procedure lock (var my_flag, his_flag :boolean);
begin
        my_flag := true;

        while his_flag do
        begin                      {if there is a clash}
                my_flag := false; {temporarily relinquish claim}
                my_flag := true;
        end
 end;
```

The revised lock procedure should mean that in the case of a clash one of the processes should be allowed to proceed, e.g.

```
Process_1                          Process_2

...                                ...
set own flag                       set own flag
test other flag - true             test other flag - true
reset own flag

                                   reset own flag

set own flag
test other flag - false
{lock now set}                     set own flag
...
<access shared data>               test other flag - true
...
...                                reset own flag
reset own flag
```

```
{lock cleared}                    set own flag
...                               test other flag - false
...                               {lock set}
                                  ...
                                  <access shared data>
                                  ...
                                  reset own flag
                                  ...
```

This solution avoids the possibility of deadlock, but it introduces another potential timing error arising from unintended synchronisation of the processes. The above example is deliberately staggered to imply that the two processes proceed at slightly different rates. However there is always the remote possibility that the two processes may be exactly synchronised so that both processes always find the other's flag set, e.g.

```
Process_1                        Process_2

...                              ...
set own flag                     set own flag
test other flag - true           test other flag - true
reset own flag                   reset own flag
set own flag                     set own flag
test other flag - true           test other flag - true
reset own flag                   reset own flag
set own flag                     set own flag
etc                              etc

...                              ...
```

Although the chances of such synchronisation occurring are slim, such situations can develop; the computer failure which delayed the launch of the first space-shuttle resulted from a synchronisation fault. The problem of synchronisation could be avoided by introducing a random time delay between a process clearing and setting its flag again.

Another problem with this protocol is that it does not guarantee that access to the shared data is fair. The protocol does not prevent one process monopolising access to the shared data and repeatedly keeping the other process delayed. It is possible for one process to leave and re-enter the critical region while the other process is resetting its own flag, e.g.·

```
Process_1                        Process_2

...
set own flag
test other flag - false
                                 ...
...                              ...
<access shared data>             set own flag
...                              test other flag - true
```

reset own flag

...

set own flag   *reset own flag*
test other flag - false

...   *set own flag*
<regain access>   *test other flag - true*

...

etc

The problem of one process, or a group of processes, preventing the progress of another process is called 'lockout'.

2.3.3. Dekker's solution

The following protocol, which solves all of these problems, is attributed to the Dutch mathematician T. Dekker; the solution gained prominence when it was presented in a famous paper by Dijkstra (1968). In addition to the two flags of the previous protocols, a third flag named *turn* is introduced to define the relative priority of the two processes. This flag may be read by both processes during the locking procedure, and the protocol also requires that both processes are capable of changing it. However, this updating is safe since it is performed only within the critical region and is therefore protected from interference. The procedures to implement the protocol are shown in Fig. 2.2. The protocol relies on the two processes using different values for the parameter *me* to identify themselves. Examples of their use are:-

Process_1
begin

     ...
     lock (flag_1, flag_2, true);

     <critical region>

     unlock (flag_1, true);
     ...

end

Process_2
begin

     ...
     lock (flag_2, flag_1, false);

     <critical section>

     unlock (flag_2, false);
     ...

end

procedure *lock* (**var** *my_flag, his_flag :boolean; me :boolean);*
begin

    my_flag := true;

    if *his_flag* **then**   {*other process in or entering region*}
        if *turn = me* **then**
              while *his_flag* **do**;   {*wait for other*}
                      {*process to leave or to concede*}
                      {*clear to enter*}

      else
              begin   {*concede to other process*}
                    my_flag := false;
                    while *turn <> me* **do**;   {*wait till*}
                        {*other process leaves*}
                    my_flag := true;
                    while *his_flag* **do**;   {*try again*}
                        {*now clear to enter*}
              end

end;

procedure *unlock* (**var** *my_flag : boolean; me : boolean);*
begin

    turn   *:=* **not** *me;*   {*priority to other process*}
    my_flag := false {*release lock*}
end;

Fig. 2.2 - Dekker's algorithm.

An example of the use of the protocol to resolve access is given below; it assumes that the value of *turn* is *true*, thus giving priority to *Process_1*. The example illustrates the most difficult case of simultaneous access attempts.

Process_1	*Process_2*
set own flag	*sets own flag*
test other flag - true	*test other flag - true*
test turn - me	*test turn - not me*
test other flag - true	*reset own flag*
test other flag - false	*test turn - not me*
{*enter region*}	*test turn - not me*
...	*test turn - not me*
{*leave region*}	*test turn - not me*

> *set turn not me*   *test turn - me*
> *reset own flag*   *set own flag*
> ...   *test other flag - false*
> ...   *{enter region}*
>   ...
>   *etc.*

If *Process_1* had attempted to reenter the region immediately after it had
exited and while *Process_2* was still executing the entry protocol, the value
of the variable *turn* would have forced it to wait for the other process, thus
ensuring fair access.

2.3.4. Summary

The previous sections have demonstrated most of the common problems associated with concurrent processes, i.e. interference, deadlock, synchronisation,
and lock-out. The difficulty of deriving a suitable protocol for just two
processes demonstrates the intricacy of the problems involved. The problems
involved in producing general solutions for *n* processes and then formally
proving them correct will not be dealt with here, but the interested reader
may find a number of solutions in the book by M. Raynal (1986).

A problem common to all of the solutions presented so far is the
inefficiency of implementation. Whenever there is contention for access the
delayed process actively examines the values of flags waiting for them to
change. This 'busy-waiting' situation is particularly wasteful of resources if
the processes are produced by multiplexing the processor between processes.
However, it can be avoided using other techniques such as semaphores, which
are the subject of the next section.

2.4. SEMAPHORES

The problems associated with using very low-level mechanisms, such as protocols with shared variables, prompted the development of higher-level conceptualisations. The first successful mechanism was the semaphore developed
by Dijkstra (1968). The semaphore is a very powerful tool which may be
used to solve most process-coordination problems. It has become so well
established as a concept that proposals for new process-coordination techniques often demonstrate their 'completeness' by showing how semaphores
may be simulated by the new methodology.

Semaphores have been established for so long now that they form an
integral part of the design of many operating systems and programming
languages. Although semaphores may be out of favour with programming
language designers, they still enjoy extensive usage.

A semaphore is defined as a non-negative integer variable for which
only two operations are defined: *P* and *V*. These are meaningful mnemonics
in Dutch, but the names *wait* and *signal* have since had widespread usage and
will be used in this book.

wait and *signal* are procedures that require a semaphore as a parameter. The manipulation of the semaphore must be implemented as an indivisible operation so that no other process may access the semaphore while it is being updated. Therefore, the procedures must either be implemented by a single, indivisible, machine-level instruction, or process scheduling must be carefully controlled during their execution. Given a semaphore *s*, the *wait* (or *P*) operation may be defined as

if *s* > *0* **then** *s* := *s* - *1*

Thus, if the value of *s* is less than or equal to zero the execution of the *wait* operation is delayed until the value of *s* is greater than zero. This definition means that *s* should never become negative. The *signal* (or *V*) operation is defined as

s := *s* + *1*

again as an indivisible operation. A *signal* operation on a semaphore with a value of zero will enable an outstanding *wait* operation to be executed. If there are a number of processes delayed while executing a *wait* operation on the same semaphore, the order in which they will complete their operation is not explicitly defined, other than that the operation of the semaphore should be fair. Fair scheduling is usually defined as not delaying a process indefinitely. In practice *wait* operations are usually completed in the order in which they are invoked.

The *wait* operation may be implemented as a busy-waiting loop, waiting for a *signal* operation. However, this may be avoided if semaphore operations are integrated into the process scheduling operations of the underlying operating system. In this case, a semaphore is usually implemented using two components, a counting field which is incremented and decremented, and the head of a queue of waiting processes. On many occasions, only the counting field is manipulated by *wait* and *signal* operations. However, if a process calls a *wait* operation when the semaphore value is zero, instead of entering a busy-waiting loop it links its process-descriptor onto the end of the list of process-descriptors which is associated with the semaphore. The process then suspends its operation (see section 1.4 and Fig. 2.3). The execution of the process is resumed later, when it will be able to complete its *wait* operation. This organisation means that the process will not waste any of the processor's resources during the delay.

If a *signal* operation finds that the semaphore has a value of zero, it checks the associated queue. If the queue is empty, indicating that there are no waiting processes, the counting field is simply incremented. If there are waiting processes, the process at the head of the queue is removed and inserted into the ready queue (again see section 1.4), with the net effect that both the *signal* and a delayed *wait* operation are completed.

A programmer can use semaphores to implement various process coordination strategies by using suitable initial values and by manipulating them

semaphore

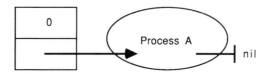

i) Process A delayed at semaphore S

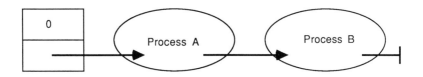

ii) Process B after executing wait (s)

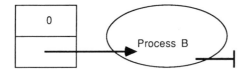

iii) After one signal (s) Process B restarted

Fig. 2.3 - Implementation of a semaphore.

using different disciplines. The following sections will examine how semaphores can be used to implement critical regions, resource control, process synchronisation, and inter-process communication.

2.4.1. Critical regions using binary semaphores

Implementing critical regions using semaphores is trivially simple, since the difficult part will already have been done during the implementation of the semaphore operations.

Each set of shared variables can be protected by an associated semaphore, *lock*, with an initial value of one. The lock and unlock functions that are required to bracket each critical section of code may be implemented directly by *wait* and *signal* operations on the semaphore. Thus each critical section will be of the form:-

```
...
wait (lock);
...
<access shared variables>
...
signal (lock);
...
```

Since the initial value of the semaphore is one, the first process to attempt to enter a critical region will execute a *wait* operation which will be completed immediately, leaving the semaphore value at zero. Any other process executing a *wait* operation will find the semaphore at zero and will, therefore, be delayed by the underlying semaphore implementation. In this way the first process gains exclusive access to shared data. On exit from the critical region each process must execute a *signal* operation. If another process is already delayed during the execution of a *wait* operation, the *signal* operation will allow it to be resumed. If there is no delayed process, the semaphore value will be set to one, so the next process to attempt to enter the critical region will not be delayed.

The correct operation of the protocol relies on adherence to three conventions throughout the program:-

(1)   the initial value of the semaphore is one.

(2)   Every critical section is bracketed by a pair of *wait* and *signal* operations.

(3)   There are no other operations performed on the semaphore.

The result is that the semaphore value is one whenever the variables are not being accessed, and the value is zero whenever they are. Since there should never have been more *signal* operations than *wait* operations, the value of the semaphore should never exceed one. A semaphore used in this fashion is referred to as a binary semaphore.

The protocol should operate correctly for any number of processes, since any number may be delayed during the *wait* operation on the same semaphore. Access to the shared data should be fair, since the operation of the semaphore is required to be fair.

2.4.2. Resource allocation using general semaphores

Semaphores provide a simple solution to the problem of controlling the allocation of a number of interchangeable resources, such as spaces in a carpark. The semaphore is used as an arbiter of the use of the pool of items, and it is given an initial value equal to the number of items available. Semaphores used with the values greater than one are referred to as 'general semaphores'. Processes wishing to use an item perform a *wait* operation on the semaphore. If an item is available, the semaphore is decremented and its new value reflects the number of items still available. The process may then proceed to use the item. When the item is no longer required, the process returns it to the pool by executing a *signal* operation which increments the value of the semaphore to reflect the increased number of available items. The pattern of usage in this mode is therefore:-

> *wait (s);*   {*acquire a resource*}
>
> ...
>
> *<use resource>*
>
> ...
>
> *signal (s);*   {*return resource to pool*}

The value of the semaphore is used to maintain a count of the number of available items; the indivisible implementation of the *wait* and *signal* operations guarantee that it is correctly updated. To implement the carpark controller would require a semaphore, *spaces_available*, which is initialised to the size of the carpark. The entry of a car to the park is recorded simply by a

> *wait (spaces_available)*

operation. This effectively allocates a space to the entering car. The departure of the car and the freeing of a space is recorded by the operation

> *signal (spaces_available).*

When demand for resources is less than the capacity of the system, any request can be immediately satisfied and processes are not delayed. Once the number of *wait* operations exceeds the number of *signal* operations by the number of resources available, all the resources will be allocated and the value of the semaphore will be zero. Subsequent *wait* operations therefore will be delayed until resources are returned and *signal* operations are performed. The fairness of the reallocation of resources once queuing becomes necessary is determined by the implementation of the semaphore.

This potential delay may be unsuitable in some situations and may necessitate convoluted or complex program design. The problem arises because the value of the semaphore is not available for direct inspection by a process. The process executing a *wait* operation has no way of determining in advance whether it will be delayed, and, having completed the operation, it will not be able to determine whether it was delayed.

This transparency of operation is useful in situations which are not time-critical, since in many cases the program is not concerned with how long it takes for the resources to be made available provided that they are available on completion of the *wait* operation. This aspect of the design reflects the original area of application of semaphores, which was to control the allocation of memory to programs in an operating system. In this environment the resources tend to be recycled rapidly so delays will not be very great, and processes tend to be independent and not time-critical.

However, the carpark is an example of an application where neither of these conditions holds. Resources may be held for a long period and at peak periods the recycling of spaces may be quite slow. Furthermore, the gate controller is interacting with the external environment and the customer expects some response within a few seconds, even if it is only a 'carpark full' message. The simple use of a *wait* operation to acquire resources for each customer on arrival is therefore not totally satisfactory since it might take minutes or even hours to respond. A possible solution would be to illuminate a 'carpark full' message before the *wait* operation. If the park is full this will serve as a response for the customer. If spaces are available the *wait* operation will be executed immediately and the process may remove the message within a few milliseconds. In this case the brief illumination of the message will probably go unnoticed by the customer. This program would be of the form:-

```
while <carpark_open> do
        begin
                <detect_customer>;
                <indicate_delay>;
                wait (spaces_available);
                <rescind_delay>;
                <admit_customer>;
        end
```

The problem with this solution lies in the fact that the customer is an autonomous agent who may decide not to wait if the carpark is full. Therefore, the gate controller should ensure that a customer is admitted before another space is requested. The program might also consider returning an unused space in such cases, by issuing a *signal* operation; i.e. the <admit_customer> operation in the program given above might become:-

if <*customer_still_waiting*> **then**
      <*admit_customer*>
else

      signal (spaces_available)

An alternative approach would be for the gate-keeper process to always keep a space 'in hand' ready to allocate to the next customer. This scheme has the advantage of detecting if the park is full before the arrival of the next customer, and avoids having to return an unwanted space. This version of the program would be of the form:-

while <*carpark_open*> **do**
      begin

            <*indicate_delay*>;
            wait (spaces_available);
            <*rescind_delay*>;
            <*await_customer*>;
            <*admit_customer*>
      end

A disadvantage of this scheme is that unused resources are being allocated to all the gate controllers. This may not be too great an overhead in a carpark where there are many more spaces than gates, but it may be unacceptable when more processes compete for more scarce resources.

Serious criticisms may also be made of the technique of illuminating and then extinguishing a message with the intention that it will go unnoticed. Firstly, this introduces time-critical interfaces between system components (carpark and customer); such interfaces are hazardous to design and to implement. Secondly, the technique is extremely inefficient since both operations will be redundant in the many cases when resources are available. Finally, it places an unnecessary strain on any electrical or mechanical components.

In summary, the general semaphore provides a simple mechanism for implementing allocation policies for interchangeable resources in time-independent situations. However, the unpredictable delays can cause problems in some situations. These may be overcome by the use of additional semaphores, but that solution introduces its own problems.

2.4.3. Using multiple semaphores

The previous section demonstrated that the general semaphore is inadequate for solving some resource allocation problems in which response time is a significant factor. The main shortcoming arises from the inability to test the value of a semaphore, which means that the behaviour of a program is unpredictable.

One solution to the problem of unpredictability is to use an integer variable to reflect the value of the semaphore; each *wait* operation must be accompanied by an operation which decrements the value of the variable, and

each *signal* operation must have accompanying increment operation performed on the variable. This allows a process to determine in advance
whether a *wait* operation will result in a delay, by inspecting the value of the
integer variable. The updating of the variable and the operations on the semaphore should be performed within a critical region to ensure that their two
values remain mutually consistent. This critical region can be implemented
with an additional binary semaphore. Thus a simple-minded, erroneous implementation of the carpark entry and exit operations might take the form:-

> *wait (lock);*
> *spaces := spaces - 1;*
> **if** *spaces < 0* **then**
>   *<indicate_delay>;*
> *wait (spaces_available);*
> **if** *<delay_indicated>* **then**
>   *<rescind_delay>;*
> *signal (lock);*

and

> *wait (lock);*
> *spaces := spaces + 1;*
> *signal (spaces_available);*
> *signal (lock);*

This scheme allows a process to inform a customer who is waiting for admis-
sion to the carpark if there will be a delay, but does not illuminate the message if the *wait* operation will be executed immediately. Unlike a semaphore,
the variable *spaces* is not restricted to being positive; when it becomes negative, its value represents the number of processes that are delayed awaiting
resources. A negative value therefore indicates that the process will be
delayed and this allows the process to determine when to illuminate the 'full'
message. However, a process cannot directly use the value of *spaces* to
determine whether it has been delayed; and some other mechanism, such as
using a private variable, must be employed to determine whether to extin-
guish the 'full' message.

  Unfortunately, this seemingly elegant scheme is fatally flawed and the
system will become 'deadlocked' as soon as the park becomes full. The
problem arises when the

> *wait (spaces_available)*

operation causes the process to be delayed until a

> *signal (spaces_available)*

operation is executed. Since the delayed process holds the exclusive access
to the critical region, no other process will pass the

> *wait (lock)*

operation and execute the required

signal (spaces_available)

operation. The situation is a deadlock since both processes are delayed waiting for the other to proceed, i.e.

entry process	*exit process*
wait(lock) - no delay	...
<indicate delay>	...
wait(space_available) - delay	*wait(lock) - delay*
...	...

To avoid deadlocks of this form, processes must be prevented from becoming delayed within a critical region and should release the mutual exclusion before executing a *wait* operation that will result in a delay. This implies that the carpark entry operation must be of the form:-

wait (lock);
spaces := spaces - 1;
if *spaces < 0* **then**
        <indicate_delay>;
signal (lock);
wait (spaces_available);
if *<delay_indicated>* **then**
        <rescind_delay>;

This would result in the sequence of operations shown below:-

entry process	*exit process*
wait(lock) - no delay	...
<indicate delay>	...
signal(lock)	...
wait(space_available) - delay	...
...	...
...	*wait(lock) - no delay*
...	*spaces := spaces + 1*
{resumed}	*signal(space_available)*
<rescind delay>	*signal(lock)*
...	...

Unfortunately, the release of mutual exclusion separates the testing of the number of spaces from the *wait* operation; therefore, other processes may interleave semaphore operations with the execution of the above sequence, giving two possible results.

The first scenario is that an exit-controlling process operates on the semaphore in the period between the time that the entry process determines that it expects to be delayed and its execution of the

wait (spaces_available)

operation. The result may be that the value of the semaphore is positive and the entry process is not delayed, meaning that a spurious 'full' message is briefly sent to the customer, i.e.

entry process	*exit process*
wait(lock) - no delay	*...*
<indicate delay>	*wait(lock) - delay*
signal(lock)	*{resumed}*
...	*spaces := spaces + 1*
...	*signal(space_available)*
wait(space_available) - no delay	*signal(lock)*
<rescind delay>	*...*
...	*...*

One purpose of introducing the variable *spaces* was to avoid this problem, and although its frequency of occurrence is greatly reduced, it is not completely cured. A total solution to the problem requires much more complex techniques.

The second interleaving scenario is potentially more serious but can be cured. It results from the interleaving of the operations of two entry processes which compete for the last available space. The second process may 'overtake' the first process and execute the

wait (spaces_available)

operation in the period between the first process releasing the mutual exclusion and executing its own

wait (spaces_available)

operation. One result is that, as in the previous scenario, the second process that expects to be delayed is allowed to continue. The second result is the unexpected delay of the first process.

entry process 1	*entry process 2*
wait(lock) - no delay	*...*
<test spaces> - ok	*wait(lock) - delay*
signal(lock)	*{resumed}*
...	*<indicate delay>*
...	*signal(lock)*
...	*wait(space_available) - no delay*
wait(space_available) - delay	*<rescind delay>*
...	*...*

This can be overcome using a more complex program structure, e.g.

wait (lock);
spaces:= spaces - 1;
if *spaces < 0* **then**
       begin
             <indicate_delay>;
             signal (lock);
             wait (spaces_available);
             <rescind_delay>;
       end
else
       begin
             wait (spaces_available);
             signal (lock);
       end

In this case the

    wait (spaces_available)

operation is included in the critical region if it will not cause a delay. The problem with this solution is that its structure is becoming so convoluted that it is difficult to design or maintain.

2.4.4. Communication and semaphores: the cycle buffer

The discussion of semaphores in the previous sections has concentrated on the synchronisation of processes, not on communication of information. The information exchanged between processes in the carpark controller was minimal, merely concerning whether space was available, not which spaces were free. This section will examine how semaphore can be used to aid communication between processes, such as between the processes in the datalogger example.

Semaphores cannot be used directly for communication. The information delivered to a process on executing a semaphore operation is minimal, and this lack resulted in the complications in implementing the carpark example. The transfer of information will therefore have to take place through the use of some shared variable while the synchronisation will be provided by semaphores. This is a classic computer science scenario known as the producer-consumer problem, which occurs in numerous applications. The most simple implementation involves coordinating the access to a single buffer variable used by two processes, the 'producer' and the 'consumer'. Since the buffer is shared, mutual exclusion of access must be provided by a semaphore (*lock*). The general form of the processes is:-

producer

while *more_data* **do**
       begin
               <produce data>
               wait (lock);
               ...
               <insert_data_into_buffer>
               ...
               signal (lock);
               signal (data_available)
       end*;*

and

consumer

while *more_data* **do**
       begin
               wait (data_available);
               wait (lock);
               ...
               <extract_data_from_buffer>;
               ...
               signal (lock);
               <consume_data>;
       end*;*

The second semaphore, *data_available*, provides the synchronisation for the the processes. It is used to reflect the availability of data and must therefore be initialised to zero, since none is initially available. If the consumer attempts to extract data before any is inserted, the value of the semaphore will be zero and the consumer will be delayed until after the producer has inserted some data and performed a *signal* operation. This reflects the logical constraint that data cannot be consumed before it is produced.

This scheme will work quite adequately using a single data variable for the buffer, provided that the rate of production is always slower than that of consumption. In this case the insertion and extraction operations take a simple form such as :-

buffer := input_data

and

output_data := buffer

This works on the assumption that the consumer is always ready for the next item and will extract it from the buffer before the producer wants to insert the next item.

However, it is an extremely bad and a potentially dangerous policy to make any assumptions about the relative speeds of processes. This is because the speeds of processes may be subject to random fluctuations as a result of the operation of scheduling policies that implement processor multiplexing, and also because a later program modification may invalidate such assumptions. In the example given above, if the consumer is delayed the producer will simply overwrite the previous data remaining in the buffer with the latest data. The problem may be overcome either by providing more synchronisation, a bigger and more complex buffering scheme, or a combination of the two.

The first solution is to provide another semaphore (say *room_available*), to reflect the availability of space in the buffer. If a single buffer variable is used, *room_available* is initialised to one, and *wait* and *signal* operations are introduced to complement the operations on *data_available*. For example:-

> *producer*

while *more_data* **do**
> **begin**
>> *<produce_data>;*
>> *wait (room_available);*
>> *wait (lock);*
>>
>> ...
>> *<insert_data_in_buffer>;*
>>
>> ...
>> *signal (lock);*
>> *signal (data_available);*
> **end;**

and

> *consumer*

while *more_data* **do**
> **begin**
>> *wait (data_available);*
>> *wait (lock);*
>>
>> ...
>> *<extract_data_from_buffer>;*
>>
>> ...
>> *signal (lock);*
>> *signal (room_available);*
>> *<consume_data>;*
> **end;**

The order of the *wait* operations is significant. Notice that the *wait* operations that are used to provide longer-term synchronisation are executed outside the critical region and so do not deadlock the system. The order of the *signal* operations is not crucial, but the above ordering is preferred on the grounds of efficiency. Other orderings involve sending a *signal* about the condition of the buffer while retaining mutual exclusion of the buffer, with the result that the resumed process would probably become delayed again immediately when it attempted to gain mutual exclusion. The process would then be resumed after the following *signal* operation. Such programs would implement logically correct behaviour, but they would be quite inefficient since delaying and resuming processes are relatively costly operations. These are minimised in the solution given.

The solution is logically symmetrical and prevents either process from proceeding at a greater rate than its partner; so the processes is quite tightly synchronised. This has the disadvantage that the maximum rate of progress of the whole system is always limited to that of the slowest process at any point in time. This may be less that the potential average rate of the slowest process if some processes have wide fluctuations in their rate of execution.

The degradation of performance can be avoided by increasing the buffer size to reduce the probability of one process being delayed waiting for the other, thus reducing the effect of fluctuations in rates of progress of individual processes. Ideally the buffer should be infinitely large to provide the greatest possible decoupling between the processes; this case will be examined before a practical realisation is considered. The general form of the program is the same as that of the first example, except that the single buffer

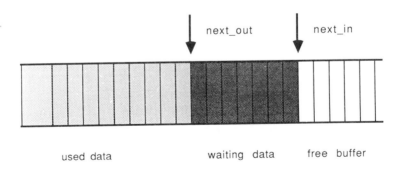

Fig. 2.4 - The unbounded buffer.

variable is replaced by an infinitely long array, and two additional variables are needed to record its usage by the producer and consumer. Both these variables are initialised to zero. These may be declared as:-

> *buf* : **array***[0..infinity]* **of** *item;*
> *next_in, next_out* : *0..infinity;*

Inserting data into the buffer involves placing it into the next array element, as indicated by the variable *next_in*, and updating *next_in* appropriately, i.e.

> *buf[next_in]* := *input_data;*
> *next_in*   := *next_in + 1;*

Data is extracted in a corresponding manner, i.e.

> *output_data* := *buf[next_out];*
> *next_out*   := *next_out + 1;*

The semaphore *data_available*, which is initialised to zero, records the number of items currently in the buffer. The organisation of the system is depicted in Fig. 2.4. Since buffer space is always available the producer proceeds at its maximum rate and is not delayed waiting for the consumer. The consumer, however, may be constrained by the semaphore to wait for the producer, since data cannot be consumed before it is produced.

In practice the infinite buffer is approximated using a fixed sized buffer and reusing the buffer elements in a cyclic manner. After accessing the last element of the array each process begins again at the first element. This organisation is depicted in Fig. 2.5. The updating of the pointer variables becomes a more complex operation, i.e.

> *next_in* := *next_in + 1;*
> **if** *next_in > max_buf* **then**
>   *next_in* := *0;*

where *max_buf* is the upper bound to the array. This can be implemented more efficiently as:-

> *next_in* := *(next_in + 1)* **modulo** *bufsize*

Where *bufsize* equals *max_buf* plus one, which is the number of elements in the array; and the **modulo** operation delivers the remainder after division, this will deliver a value in the range zero to *max_buf*. This operation is very efficient to implement at machine level if 'round' binary numbers are used, such as 8 or 256. The lower bound of the array was chosen to be zero to allow for this optimisation.

With a limited buffer capacity, it is possible that the producer may proceed so much faster than the consumer that all the buffer becomes full. The producer must therefore be prevented from overwriting data in the buffer before it it consumed, so the semaphore *room_available* is again required, this

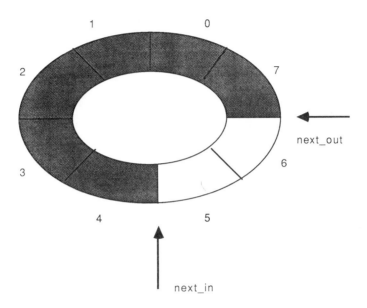

Fig. 2.5 - A cyclic buffer.

time initialised to *bufsize* to indicate the available space. Cyclic buffers are very important tools for concurrent programming and their operation should be clearly understood. Their implementation using semaphores is summarised in Fig. 2.6. With a cyclic buffer, each process may become delayed waiting for the other; however, the two processes are much less tightly coupled than when a single buffer variable is used, and there is room for variations in their rates of progress. The size of the variations which may occur before the other process is affected depends on the size of the buffer. The rate of progress of the system will be dependent on the slowest average rate of processing of a buffer-full of data, not on the rate of processing of individual data items.

2.4.5. Summary of semaphores

The primitive nature of the semaphore means that this one facility may be employed in a variety of protocols to solve most problems of process coordination. By employing different patterns of usage and different initialisations, semaphores can provide mutual exclusion, resource allocation, process

constant
  max_buf = 100;
  bufsize = max_buf + 1;

variables
  buf : **array***[0..max_buf]* **of** *item;*
  next_in, next_out : 0..max_buf;
  lock   : binary semaphore initially 1;
  data_available : semaphore initially 0;
  room_available : semaphore initially bufsize;

Producer Process;

  ...
while *more_data* **do**
        begin
                <produce data>;
                wait (room_available);   {updating free buffer space}
                wait (lock);   {for mutual exclusion}
                buf[next_in]   := item; {insert data}
                next_in   := (next_in + 1) **modulo** *bufsize;*
                signal (lock);   {release mutual exclusion}
                signal (data_available)   {update data count}
        end;

Consumer Process

  ...
while *more_data* **do**
        begin
                wait (data_available);   {wait for producer}
                wait (lock);   {for mutual exclusion}
                data   := buf[next_out];{extract data}
                next_out := (next_out + 1) **modulo** *bufsize;*
                signal (lock);   {release mutual exclusion}
                signal (room_available); {update space count}
                <consume_data>;
        end;

Fig. 2.6 - Program code of a cyclic buffer.

synchronisation and interprocess communication.

This power is also the semaphore's weakness. The programs are very difficult to understand and the fact that a semaphore may be used for all of these functions compounds the difficulties. Another problem is that operations on the semaphore variables are widely distributed throughout the program, making it difficult to understand or modify the use of a semaphore.

The general nature of semaphores means that a semaphore operation within a program has very little 'semantic content' to be checked by a compiler. Initially this may be seen as an advantage since it means that incorporating semaphores into an existing language is very simple. However, this is outweighed by the disadvantage that the compiler is very limited in the error-checking that it can perform. Subsequent language developments have tended to provide more restricted and specialised constructs. These make programs more reliable, comprehensive and checkable, at the expense of greater effort in the development of the compiler.

2.5. SUMMARY

To reflect the asynchronous structures of the systems they model or control, concurrent programs also emphasise asynchronous operation and non-determinism. This chapter introduced the use of multiple independent processes which interact both synchronously and asynchronously. Concurrent programs should make the minimum possible assumptions about absolute or relative speeds of processes. It is preferable to assume only that the rate of progress of each process is greater than zero. This should make the programs independent of the timing of the underlying hardware or operating system, and therefore more portable.

The first technique examined in this chapter was the use of shared memory. This is essentially an asynchronous mechanism. The processes involved are independent, and synchronisation must be imposed by explicitly implementing protocols within the program. The implementation presented used the technique of 'polling'. Processes determine the status of the system by repeatedly examining, or polling, the value of significant variables. In general, polling is very wasteful of processing resources and it should be employed only if there is nothing else for the processor to be doing, or if the delay is predicted to be so short that process context switching is not worthwhile. The examination of the use of shared memory introduced the many potential synchronisation problems which may arise: deadlock, synchronisation and starvation.

The inefficiencies and difficulty of use of shared memory constructs prompted the development of other mechanisms such as the semaphore. Semaphores are usually designed to operate in conjunction with some process-scheduling mechanism and therefore, they make much more efficient use of the processor than does a polling system. Semaphores offer both asynchronous and synchronous coordination depending on the manner of their use.

Their use to implement mutual exclusion or for controlling resource allocation is essentially asynchronous. However, they can also be programmed to provide more explicit synchronisation if a process expects to be delayed on a *wait* operation until a *signal* operation is performed by another process.

The primitive methodologies introduced in this chapter have two major weaknesses.

(1)   The coordination of access to shared data is not explicitly provided and it depends on the programmer for its correct implementation. This may lead to many difficult program errors since calls to the synchronisation protocol may be widely distributed throughout the program.

(2)   The mechanisms fail to distinguish the two modes of process coordination: communication and synchronisation. The mechanisms are also combined with program data variables, resulting in extremely complex and tortuous programs that are very difficult to design and maintain.

After the development of semaphores, methodologies for producing concurrent programs developed into two major schools. Both concentrate on limiting access to shared data.

The first school formalised the concept of critical regions into a language construct called a monitor. Monitors are program modules which encapsulate data structures together with procedures by which the variables may be accessed by the program's processes. Mutual exclusion of access to monitor data is provided automatically by the compiler and the language's run-time support package. Methodologies of this form are often referred to as procedure-oriented. The languages Concurrent Pascal and Modula, amongst others, implement this methodology.

The second methodology prohibits the use of shared data by the programmer. Instead all application-level process coordination is implemented using a message-passing facility that is provided by the support software. In this way all of the problems associated with the use of shared data are kept within the language-implementation or operating system kernel. The form of the message facility that is provided may vary on a number of dimensions giving a wide spectrum of implementations.

In fact, the two methods are not in principle incompatible and a further school promoting operation-oriented methodologies has since been developed which combines aspects of both.

Part II of the book considers each of these three schools in turn in greater detail.

PART II

The Models

The second part of the book examines the three paradigms of structuring programs that have emerged. Monitor systems, message systems, and remote operations are each covered in separate chapters. The final chapter of this part of the book interrelates the different program styles.

3

Procedure Based
Interaction : Monitors

3.1. INTRODUCTION

Chapter 2 examined problems associated with attempts to share data or to communicate between processes. The use of semaphores to implement mutual exclusion within critical regions was covered in some detail. One drawback of using semaphores is that their dispersal throughout the program greatly impedes its comprehension or modification. An early improvement on the semaphore methodology was the introduction of a notation to identify critical regions within the program (Brinch Hansen, 1973). The programmer was expected to identify and delineate the critical regions within the program text, and the compiler automatically generated semaphores and appropriate operations to implement mutual exclusion. Whilst this is a great improvement, it still relies on the programmer to identify the regions, which remain distributed throughout the program.

From the concept of regions there rapidly evolved the idea of a monitor which encapsulates the shared data together with any operations defined for it, where these operations are expressed as procedures (Hoare, 1974). Concurrent Pascal (CP) (Brinch Hansen, 1975) was the first language to implement monitors and thus it will be used here to examine the use of the monitor concept and some of its associated problems. Once the ideas and difficulties are understood, the solutions adopted in other monitor-based languages will be examined as well as some enhancements to the basic concepts.

3.2. STRUCTURE OF CONCURRENT PASCAL PROGRAMS

The monitor concept introduced a major departure from the liberal scope rules of its forerunners, the block structured languages such as Pascal or PL/I. These languages gave processes free access to global variables by default. The programmer was then expected to impose discipline on the use of the variables by means of protocols within the program. In contrast, a CP program consists of a series of 'system components' defining their own disjoint address spaces. By default all variables are private, and the programmer must explicitly define the possible routes for communication or interaction.

A CP program is composed of three types of system components: **processes**, **monitors** and **classes**.

(1)   **Processes** correspond closely with the concept of a process introduced earlier in this book. They consist of local variables that are private to the process and the program statements that may operate on them. The processes are the active part of the system.

(2)   **Monitors** provide the only means by which the processes may coordinate their operation. The structure of a monitor definition is similar to a that of a definition of process, consisting of private variables and the procedures by which they may be accessed. A monitor is a passive object which is manipulated by those processes which are entitled to call the the procedures of the monitor. Mutual exclusion of access to the variables of a monitor is enforced by the underlying implementation, which schedules the execution of the monitor's procedures.

(3)   **Classes** are similar to monitors and provide 'abstract data structures' consisting of data and procedures. However, restrictions on their definition and use mean that they are never accessible to more than one process at a time, so the overhead of establishing mutual exclusion is avoided. The main purpose of classes is program optimisation and they will be ignored in the following discussion.

By default processes may *not* access a monitor; permission to do so must be *explicitly* granted in its 'access rights'.

CP is based extensively on standard Pascal and the structure of process and monitor definitions is very similar to that of procedure definitions. They may contain constant and type definitions, variable and procedure declarations, and are concluded by a sequence of statements. A limitation of the language is the lack of reference or pointer variables and of recursive procedure calls. These restrictions allow the maximum storage requirements of a system component to be determined during compilation so that an adequate area of memory may be allocated to each system component when it is initialised. This policy avoids the problems of dynamic storage allocation. The final sequence of statements of a monitor may be used to initialise its variables before they are accessed by other system components; in a process the statements define its operation.

Within a monitor, some procedures or functions may be defined as **entry** routines. These routines may be called by another system component, but they are not accessible from within the monitor itself. The run-time system enforces mutual exclusion of execution of entries to a system component.

Process and monitor definitions may be parametrised in an analogous manner to procedure parameter definitions. Parameter definitions consist of a sequence of variable names and their types; suitable values must be supplied when the component is initialised. A parameter identified as a simple variable requires a constant value for its initial value. A parameter referring to monitor type must be initialised with a reference to a monitor of the specified type. The supplied parameters specify the access rights to other system components. A parameter's entry procedures may be invoked by specifying the name of both the parameter and of the procedure, connected by a dot (.). Parameters to the procedure are given in the usual manner, i.e.

<monitor_name>.<procedure_name> (<actual_parameters>);

The structure of a monitor-based solution to the carpark problem is outlined below. The variable *spaces* is contained in a monitor *space_control* with two entry procedures:-

```
space_control = monitor;
const
        max_spaces = 100;

var
        spaces : 0..max_spaces;


        procedure entry arrive;
        begin
                spaces := spaces - 1;
        end;


        procedure entry depart;
        begin
                spaces := spaces + 1;
        end;

begin
        spaces := max_spaces
end;
```

This simple solution ignores the problem of what happens when the carpark
becomes full, but it illustrates the structure of a monitor. Notice the initialisation of *spaces* in the final statement. This monitor may then be accessed by
processes controlling the entrance and exit gates:-

      entrance_control = **process** *(tally : space_control);*

   begin
         cycle
                  <await_customer>;
                  tally.arrive;
                  <admit_customer>;
         end;
   end; *{entrance_control}*

      exit_control = **process** *(tally : space_control);*

   begin
         cycle
                  <detect_leaver>;
                  tally.depart;
                  <dismiss_leaver>;
         end;
   end; *{exit_control}*

Both of these processes have access to the monitor and invoke its procedures
to update the common data in *spaces*. The

   cycle
         <sequence_of_statements>
   end

construct indicates the indefinite repetition of the enclosed statements. The
above process definitions are degenerate cases; such definitions would normally include local variable and procedure declarations.

      In CP, system variables are treated as a special form of structured vari-
able. The above definitions are *type-definitions*; they define new types of system objects. The actual variables, called 'system components', are declared
in the usual way later in the program and they are initialised in an **init** statement at the end of the program. The overall shape of the program is given in
Fig. 3.1. Since system components are defined in type-definitions, it is possible to declare a number of similar *entrance_control* and *exit_control*
processes to control the gates. These definitions need to be refined to include
an additional parameter to identify ·to the process which gate it controls, so
that the process can communicate with the correct interface hardware.

```
type {define system types}

        space_control = monitor;
                ...
                procedure entry arrive;
                ...
                procedure entry depart;
                ...
        begin
                ...
        end; {space_control}


        entrance_control = process (tally: space_control; me: integer);
                ...
                tally.arrive;    {call monitor procedure}
                ...
        end; {entrance_control}


        exit_control = process (tally : space_control; me: integer);
                ...
        end; {exit_control}


var {declare system components}
        counter           : space_control;
        wayin1, wayin2 : entrance_control;
        wayout1, wayout2: exit_control;


begin {initialise components}
        init
                counter,
                wayin1(counter, 1),
                wayin2(counter, 2),
                wayout1(counter, 1),
                wayout2(counter, 2)
end.
```

Fig. 3.1 - Outline of carpark controller in CP.

This example demonstrates how monitors may provide coordination where only mutual exclusion is required. This is provided by the underlying implementation which ensures mutual exclusion of access to a monitor. If several processes attempt to access the *space_control* simultaneously, some would be delayed to ensure that the procedures are executed sequentially. CP employs a fifo (first in first out) discipline for monitor entry, so the access to a monitor is fair and should not result in process starvation. Longer term process synchronisation, such as that required when the carpark is full, requires a separate mechanism which will be examined in section 3.2.2.

3.2.1. Monitor invariants

For a program to be reliable or modifiable, the data variables should be related in some coherent manner. However, identifying and maintaining the coherence becomes increasingly complex with the size of the program, so the rate of production of a program (in terms of tested and correct lines of program per programmer per day) falls dramatically as the program size increases. A small but non-trivial program may be produced at about 100 lines per day, which may fall to 3 lines per day for large real-time programs. The need to control this increase in complexity prompted the development of the modularised languages such as CP.

The processes and monitors are largely self-contained, independent units of quite small size. The first significant program written in CP was the Solo operating system (Brinch Hansen, 1977); it is composed of 23 component types of approximately 60 lines each. Controlling the use of the variables within each of these modules is obviously much simpler than it would have been if it were written as a single monolithic program.

The notion of 'data coherence' may be formalised by defining some invariant condition, *I*, which must be maintained for the variables within a monitor. It may not be possible to maintain *I* during the manipulation of monitor variables, but any process entering a monitor should be able to assume that the invariant holds. *I* must therefore be established by the monitor's initialisation statements and by each process before it relinquishes its exclusive hold on the monitor. The invariant for the *space_control* monitor in the previous section is:-

   (spaces >= 0) **and** *(spaces <= max_spaces)*

i.e. no process should leave the monitor with a negative number of spaces available or with more spaces recorded as available then actually exist. This invariant is established by the initialisation of *spaces*, but the weakness of this particular monitor's design may be seen in the fact that the invariant is never established or maintained within the code of the entry procedures. The above invariant is a particularly simple example, because the monitor contains only one variable. Normally an invariant would interrelate a collection of variables, as the example of a circular buffer will demonstrate in the next section.

Generally, invariants enjoy only the status of design tool; only a few experimental systems require the programmer to express them formally or explicitly within a program.

3.2.2. Synchronisation

Monitors by themselves only provide mutual exclusion. Since their operation is essentially asynchronous and random they cannot provide the synchronisation necessary to control a pool of re-usable resources, such as in the carpark example, or to handle the synchronised communication through a buffer required by the data-logger. A wide variety of techniques have been proposed to provide this synchronisation. This section will examine the particular implementation adopted by CP. Some of the alternative proposals will be reviewed later in the chapter.

In CP, synchronisation is provided by a new variable type, the *queue*. *Queues* may only be declared as permanent variables within a monitor; i.e. as a global variable, not local to a procedure. They are manipulated only by three standard routines defined to operate on them: *delay, continue* and *empty*. Given a *queue* variable q, the procedure call

   delay (q)

results in the calling process being suspended until another process executes the complementary procedure

   continue (q)

which results in the former process resuming its operation. In practice q is used to store the process-id of the delayed process. A *queue* variable is only capable of storing a single process-id, so a *delay* operation invoked on a non-empty *queue* is an error and its effect is undefined. The rationale for this design is that it provides the programmer with a basic tool which can be implemented very efficiently with minimum overhead. The programmer is then free to implement his own scheduling policies by declaring arrays of *queues* and defining the algorithms which determine the order in which any *delay* or *continue* operations are invoked.

The operation of *queues* differ from semaphores since there is no associated counting field to record any *continue* operations that are issued when there is no waiting process. A *continue* operation on an empty *queue* is simply a null operation and has no effect. This means that a *delay* operation always results in the process suspending its operation.

The boolean function *empty(q)* allows a process to determine the status of a *queue* variable.

Queue variables can be accessed only within the monitor in which they are declared, so a process operating on a *queue* must hold exclusive access to the monitor at the time of execution. A *delay* operation automatically releases the process' exclusive hold on the monitor, otherwise no other process could enter to issue the corresponding *continue* operation. Since the delaying process is effectively leaving the monitor and allowing another to enter, the monitor invariant, *I*, should be established at this point, as well as on procedure exit.

Conceptually each *queue* variable should be associated with some condition, say *B*, concerning the variables of the monitor which is more stringent than the invariant. An example might be that the carpark is not full, so *spaces* is greater than zero. A process delayed in a *queue* should be able to assume that, when it resumes its operation, this condition, *B*, also holds, in addition to the invariant, *I*. This may be expressed:-

> *I*   {*await B*}   *I* and *B*

Before executing a *continue* operation a process should establish the associated condition, but should not assume that the condition holds afterwards, since the resumed process may immediately invalidate the condition, i.e.

> *I* and *B* {*indicate B*}   *I*

This is illustrated in the carpark example where a process may return a free space and indicate that the carpark is no longer full, but the space may be immediately allocated to a waiting process so the park is again full.

When the *continue* operation is invoked, the delayed process should be resumed immediately; this ensures that the condition, *B*, associated with the *queue*, is not invalidated before the process is resumed. This means that there are two processes active within the monitor. The solution to this problem adopted by CP is to combine an exit from the monitor with the *continue* operation. Since control of the monitor is relinquished at this point, the invariant should first be established, and the *continue* operation is usually the last statement of the procedure. The following modified structure of the carpark monitor *space_control* illustrates the use of *queues*, it allows for the case when the park becomes full; the example assumes that there is only one *entrance_control* process.

```
space_control = monitor; {allows for full park}

const
        max_spaces = 100;

var
        spaces          : 0.. max_spaces;
        space_ready     : queue;

        procedure entry arrive;
        begin
                if spaces = 0 then
                        delay (space_ready);
                spaces := spaces - 1
```

end*;*

procedure entry *depart;*
begin

        spaces := spaces + 1;
        continue (space_ready)
end*;*

begin

        spaces := max_spaces
end*;*

Notice that the procedure *depart* always executes a *continue* operation, since if no process is delayed it will have no effect.

The *arrive* procedure could be extended to indicate to a waiting customer when the park is full, for example:-

procedure entry *arrive;*
begin

        if *spaces = 0* **then**
            begin

                <indicate_delay>;
                delay (space_ready);
                <rescind_delay>;

            end*;*
        spaces := spaces - 1;
end*;*

This implementation is considerably simpler than the semaphore-based solution of section 2.4.3, since the semantics of **monitors** and *queues* closely model the domain to which they are applied. This example could be generalised to allow for multiple entries at this point; however, consideration will be delayed until the next section where it serves to illustrate a problem of monitors.

The process-monitor format is also easily applied to the data-logger example of section 2.2. The three functions of data-capture, analysis and storage can be implemented as separate processes. These communicate through two cyclic buffers implemented as monitors using a similar algorithm to the semaphore implementation of section 2.4.4, the program is given in Fig. 3.2.

Since both programs realise the same algorithm it is not surprising that the two implementations are very similar. The semaphore *lock*, which provides mutual exclusion, is implemented automatically by the monitor entry mechanism. The semaphores *data_available* and *room_available* provide synchronisation and their counting fields keeps track of buffer usage. The synchronisation function is performed by the corresponding *queues*:

```
cyclic_buffer = monitor;

const
        max_buf = 100
        bufsize = 101; {max_buf + 1}

var
        buf : array[0..max_buf] of object;
        next_in, next_out         : 0..max_buf;
        count                     : 0..bufsize;
        data_ready, room_ready  : queue;

        procedure entry produce (item : object);
        begin
                if count = bufsize then
                        delay (room_ready);
                buf[next_in]      := item;
                next_in           := (next_in  + 1) mod bufsize;
                count             := count + 1;
                continue (data_ready)
        end;

        procedure entry consume (var data : object);
        begin
                if count = 0 then
                        delay (data_ready);
                data              := buf[next_out];
                next_out          := (next_out + 1) mod bufsize;
                count             := count - 1;
                continue (room_ready)
        end;

begin {initialise}
        next_in  := 0;
        next_out := 0;
        count    := 0
end;   {cyclic_buffer}
```

Fig. 3.2 - Cyclic buffer programmed in CP.

data_ready and *room_ready*. However, since *queues* are primitive objects they must be supplemented by the variable *count*, the two conditional statements to test its value, and two statements to update its value.

A monitor invariant of the buffer is:-

next_in = (next_out + count) **mod** *bufsize*

i.e. the input pointer is ahead of the output pointer by the number of items in the buffer. This is established in the initialisation:-

$0 = (0 + 0)$

It is then maintained by the two procedures: *produce* adds 1 to both sides of the equation, *consume* adds 1 to, and subtracts 1 from, the terms in parentheses. A second invariant is also required to ensure the buffer's correct functioning:-

(count >= 0) **and** *(count <= bufsize)*

i.e. data may not be extracted before it is inserted and it must not overflow. These conditions are enforced using the *queue* variables. The condition associated with *room_ready* is

count < bufsize

and *data_ready* requires that

count > 0

Establishing that these conditions hold at the beginning of the procedures means that the invariant will hold throughout their subsequent execution. Identifying and validating invariants in this manner can provide a high degree of confidence in the correct functioning of a monitor.

3.2.3. Nested monitors

Fundamental to the monitor concept is the belief that complex systems can be built in a modular fashion. Each module should be conceptually simple and well defined, and present an integrated interface to the rest of the system. It should be possible for monitors to call the procedures of others which implement different or more fundamental concepts. However, it is difficult to integrate the simple nesting of monitor calls with the requirement for mutual exclusion.

The following example in CP illustrates the general problem. Since a *queue* variable can hold only one process-id, it would be useful to define a monitor, *fifo*, to provide a multiple queue from an array of *queues* which may be used by other monitors. For instance, it could serve the *space_control* monitor of a multi-gated carpark when it becomes full. The implementation and use of *fifo* is outlined in Fig. 3.3, and the structure of the program is illustrated in Fig. 3.4. This structure is logical and easy to follow, and the *fifo* monitor provides an enhanced facility for use by other system

```
const
        max_gates = 5;
type

fifo = monitor;
    var
        bufq : array[0..max_gates] of queue;
        last_in, last_out, waiting : 0..max_gates;

        procedure entry fdelay;
        begin
                waiting := waiting + 1;
                last_in   := (last_in + 1) mod (max_gates + 1);
                delay (bufq[last_in])
        end;

        procedure entry fcontinue;
        begin
        if waiting > 0 then
                begin
                        waiting   := waiting - 1;
                        last_out := (last_out + 1) mod (max_gates+1);
                        continue (bufq[last_out])
                {continue must be last statement as forces exit!}
                end
        end;

begin
        waiting  := 0;
        last_in  := 0;
        last_out := 0;
end;    {fifo}


space_control = monitor (fqueue : fifo);
var
        spaces : 0..max_spaces;

        procedure entry arrive;
        begin
                if spaces = 0 then
                        fqueue.fdelay; {wait in fifo}
                spaces := spaces - 1
        end;
```

procedure entry *depart;*
begin
       spaces := spaces + 1;
       fqueue.fcontinue
end;

begin
       spaces := max_spaces
end;   *{space_control}*

Fig. 3.3 - The nested monitor problem.

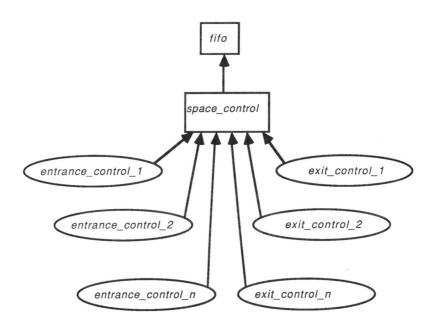

Fig. 3.4 - Structure of the carpark controller leading to deadlock.

components. However, this example raises the question of when to relinquish the exclusive hold of the monitor *space_control* while the process calls *fifo*, especially if the process delays in *fifo*. In a normal CP monitor, a process releases its exclusive hold on a *delay* operation to allow another process access to the *queue* and to execute the *continue* operation. However, with a nested structure access to a series of monitors is required in order to reference the *queue*.

Four policies for the release of mutual exclusion have been suggested within the traditional monitor paradigm.

(1)   Maintain exclusive access to all monitors and release exclusion on the current monitor only on a *delay* operation.

(2)   Maintain exclusion on a nested call, but release exclusive access to all monitors on *delay* operations.

(3)   Always release exclusive access to the current monitor on a nested call to another monitor.

(4)   Prohibit nested calls.

The 'current monitor release' policy (1) is adopted in CP. This is simple to implement but it may lead to deadlock with a nested structure. When the carpark is full, an *entrance_control* process would call *space_control*, then *fifo* and then *delay*, releasing its exclusive hold on *fifo* but not *space_control*. The *exit_control* process would therefore be prevented from entering *space_control* and so never access *fifo*. The system would be deadlocked. To avoid this, the programmer must structure the program so that delays in nested monitors do not occur unless there is an alternative route by which the *queue* will be accessed. This sometimes forces rather inelegant compromises upon a program's design; for instance, *fifo* could be incorporated into *space_control*, but this reduces the modularity of the design and means that other instances of *fifo* could not be used elsewhere in the program. An alternative would be to maintain two monitors corresponding to *space_control* and *fifo*, and require that the processes using them will observe a suitable protocol for their use. An *entrance_control* process that finds the carpark is full would have to leave *space_control* and then enter *fifo* and delay. On resumption it would need to re-enter *space_control* and attempt to claim a space, but it may have been pre-empted by another *entrance_control* and have to wait again. The *exit_control* processes would need to examine the value of the variable *spaces* each time to determine whether it needs to call *fifo* to resume a waiting *entrance_control*. This would lead to a program structure represented in Fig. 3.5.

The problems of deadlock are avoided by the second and third approaches, which release all mutual exclusion. These policies also provide greater potential for concurrency, at the cost of having to re-establish mutual exclusion when a process resumes its execution after a *delay* operation or when it returns from a nested monitor call. For both approaches it is necessary to establish the monitor's invariant on a call to another monitor. The

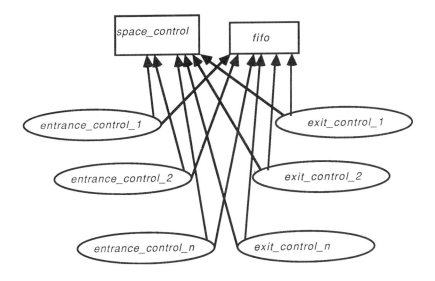

Fig. 3.5 - Possible carpark control structure.

release of exclusion while the process is in a nested monitor means that it is necessary to prohibit the use of reference parameters in monitor procedure calls. Otherwise reference parameters would allow the process to manipulate monitor variables indirectly while another process occupied the monitor. These policies have been employed during the implementation of some experimental operating systems, but have not been realised in the major monitor-based languages.

The fourth policy, that of prohibiting nested monitor calls, has been adopted in some languages but it restricts the structuring of programs.

The problems are caused in part by attempting to employ a single linguistic construct and the single simple implementation policy of mutual exclusion to provide the facilities for all system designs. This approach has great appeal for language designers and implementors, but it is restrictive for the sophisticated programmer. Language designers may choose to follow one of three routes at this point:-

(1)   Increase the complexity and sophistication of language designs to provide additional special constructs tailored to providing particular facilities.

(2)   Provide tools of a more basic nature which the programmer may use to implement suitable constructs and policies. This offers more flexibility but requires more work and offers less support for the applications programmer.

(3)   Try to develop a different methodology, such as message passing.

Unfortunately, whichever course is followed, the problems of structuring complex systems and avoiding deadlock persist in some guise.

3.2.4. Implementation of CP

CP was initially implemented to run directly on PDP 11 processors. Since one aim of the project was to develop an operating system, no underlying software support was assumed. Most of the implementation was programmed in Pascal and the system was designed with portability in mind. This has facilitated the subsequent implementation of the language on a number of machines, sometimes running under their own operating systems.

The initial implementation was based on a small set of kernel routines written in assembly code which provided three major functions:-

(1)   The provision of multiple processes by processor multiplexing.

(2)   The implementation of mutual exclusion of monitor access.

(3)   The interface to peripheral devices.

These routines are called by the language implementation routines, which are invoked by the code produced by the compiler from the source code.

The compiler generates code for all of the processes, reserves the data area for the monitor variables, and generates the code for an initial process. When a program is loaded, it initialises the monitor variables, which are permanently allocated space in an area of memory accessible to all processes. The processes are then initialised. A fixed data area is allocated for each process stack, the size of the area for each process may be determined by the compiler. This area is never reclaimed, even if the process terminates. A process-descriptor is then generated within the kernel which is linked into the 'ready queue' of processes waiting to be allocated. Once all the processes have been generated, the initial process terminates but the kernel continues to multiplex the processor between the processes in the ready queue on a time-sliced basis.

Monitors, like processes, consist of data within the program area and an associated control structure within the kernel. When the monitor is initialised, a special word in the data area, the gate, is initialised to refer to the control structure. This control structure is similar to a semaphore and consists of a boolean variable defining when the monitor is in use, and the head of a queue of waiting processes. To enter a monitor, a process calls a kernel routine passing the gate address as a parameter. If the monitor is free the gate is updated to reflect the change of status, and the process continues. If the monitor is occupied, the process attaches its descriptor to the end of the monitor's queue and the processor is multiplexed to a ready process.

When a process leaves a monitor it examines the monitor gate. If other processes are found to be waiting to enter, a descriptor is removed from the front of the gate's queue and is attached to the ready queue. When the process is selected to run it will automatically enter the monitor. If there are no waiting processes the gate is simply updated to indicate that the monitor is free.

The *queue* variables declared within a monitor are implemented as a single variable within the program's data space, and can be used to store a reference to a process. On a *delay* operation the process stores a reference to its descriptor in the *queue*, frees the monitor by manipulating the gate and then relinquishes the processor to the next ready process. On a *continue* operation, the reference to the descriptor of the delayed process is retrieved from the *queue* and is inserted into the ready queue so that it will resume its execution within the monitor. The process that initiates the action is forced to exit from the monitor.

Since the kernel contains some shared data structures, in the form of process queues and monitor gates, which may be manipulated by the various user-processes, the kernel operations must be implemented as indivisible operations and ordinary processor multiplexing is suspended during their execution. Thus the kernel is itself implemented as a monitor.

CP **processes** may not directly access peripheral devices, but must issue requests using the standard procedure *doio*. This results in a request being passed to the kernel. The kernel then interfaces to the device and returns the results to the user process. The advantages of the scheme are that it provides a uniform interface between the user program and the peripheral devices, and that it hides the details of the device handling within the kernel. The disadvantages of the scheme are that the device handling must be done in assembly code, which is more difficult than using a high level language, and that adding a new device to the system requires the modification of the kernel. The topic of device interfacing is examined in more detail in Chapter 7.

3.2.5. Summary of CP

CP was developed in the period from 1972 to 1975 and represents the first attempt to integrate the concepts of processes and monitors into a language. The basic structure of CP is very similar to Pascal: the processes and monitors are integrated into the language as new 'structured types', which take the form of a program block. Within a type-definition the usual scope rules of block structured languages apply, except for monitor procedures declared as entries, which can be accessed only from other system components. System components may access only those components to which they are explicitly granted access in their parameter section. This provides quite tight control of access and security within the program.

Long term synchronisation of processes is provided by the simple *queue* variable, in which a single process may be suspended, and the associated *delay* and *continue* operations. The *delay* operation releases the exclusive hold of the immediately enclosing monitor, but not of any more global monitors in the case of a nested call. The *continue* operation forces the running process to exit from the monitor; it must, therefore, be the last logical operation within a monitor procedure.

As the first attempt to define a controlled concurrent language, CP is quite successful. The introduction of system components as type definitions is a powerful idea, since multiple instances of objects, such as terminal interfaces, can be easily provided. The major criticisms have focussed on the language's static nature and the difficulty of introducing new peripheral devices into a system.

3.3. COMPARISON OF MONITOR-BASED LANGUAGES

A major success of CP is the amount of related research and development that it stimulated by providing a suitable notation and a framework for discussion of the issues. As well as prompting its own refinements and modifications, it also stimulated and influenced the development of some related languages. This section will examine the design decisions taken in three of these languages:-

Concurrent Euclid
Mesa
Modula

Each of these languages have been used to implement substantial projects such as operating systems. A number of other similar languages are also available commercially.

3.3.1. Concurrent Euclid

Concurrent Euclid (CE) (Holt, 1983), was defined in 1980 as a systems programming language based on the language Euclid. It has been implemented on a range of of machines from micros to mainframes, and is available from the University of Toronto. Euclid was a refinement of Pascal, and was intended to aid the development of verification techniques. CE then added features necessary for concurrency and systems programming.

The basic program unit in CE is the module, which corresponds to a program block: it packages together procedures and functions with their data variables. The visibility of program identifiers does not follow the liberal scope rules of Pascal; identifiers must be explicitly exported from a module, and be imported into another, before they may be used. To call a procedure in another module both identifiers must be given, as in CP, i.e.

<module_id>.<procedure_id> (<parameters>)

Processes and monitors are introduced as special forms of global modules, which are identified by reserved words. Only exported procedures may be accessed from outside a monitor, and mutual exclusion of access is provided by the underlying implementation. The access rights of a process are restricted to those modules that are explicitly imported. An outline of the carpark controller programmed in CE is given in Fig. 3.6. Once the program is loaded into the machine, the initialisation procedures of the monitors are executed and then the processes are executed concurrently.

Module definitions are effectively variable declarations and not type definitions, so it is not possible to define a collection of similar monitors or processes. However, it is possible to define global procedures that can be shared by processes to save replicating all the code.

Long term synchronisation is provided by *condition* variables. These are similar to CP *queues*, but allow any number of processes to *wait* in the same *condition*. A *wait* operation releases a process' exclusive access to the monitor. A *signal* operation on a *condition* will resume one process from the queue; the order of resumption is required to be fair, but not necessarily fifo. A *signal* operation immediately resumes a waiting process if there is one; in this case the signalling process is temporarily suspended but it will later resume its execution of the monitor. However, it is possible that other processes may gain access to the monitor before a signalling process resumes, so no assumptions about the state of the monitor may be made after a *signal* operation. CE also provides *priority conditions* which allow waiting processes to specify their priority; a *signal* then resumes the highest priority waiting process, their operation obviously may not be fair. Like CP, CE allows nested monitor calls and employs the 'current monitor release' protocol which introduces the potential for deadlock.

CE allows a program to access peripheral devices directly; it also allows program modules to be compiled individually and stored in libraries or incorporated into a program. In combination these mechanisms mean that library routines can provide extensive support for accessing standard devices but the programmer can easily introduce routines to support special devices.

CE provides a more dynamic environment than CP by providing a form of pointer or reference variable. Unfortunately, it retains a static program structure in terms of modules and, therefore, of processes and monitors. CE overcame most of the inadequacies of CP, but the static program structure remains a major shortcoming.

3.3.2. Mesa

The language Mesa (Lampson, 1980) was developed in the late 1970s to implement operating systems and applications software for the Xerox personal computers. Mesa aims to be more dynamic than CP and CE, and allows the dynamic creation of processes and monitors. It also addresses error handling and recovery, problems which are frequently ignored by designers of other

```
var carpark : module

        var space_control : monitor
                exports (arrive, depart)
                const
                        max_spaces = 100
                var
                        spaces          : SignedInt
                        space_ready     : condition

                procedure Arrive =
                        imports (var spaces, space_ready)
                        begin
                                if spaces = 0 then
                                        wait (space_ready);
                                spaces := spaces - 1
                        end Arrive

                procedure Depart =
                        imports (var spaces, space_ready)
                        begin
                                spaces := spaces + 1;
                                if spaces = 1 then
                                        signal (space_ready);
                        end Depart

                initially
                        imports (var spaces, max_spaces)
                        begin
                                spaces := max_spaces
                        end

        end monitor


        process Entrance_control
                imports (var space_control)
                begin
                        loop
                                <await_customer>;
                                space_control.arrive;
                                <admit_customer>;
                        end loop
                end Entrance_control
```

```
process Exit_control
        imports (var space_control)
        begin
              loop
                     <detect_leaver>;
                     space_control.depart;
                     <dismiss_leaver>;
              end loop
        end Exit_control

end module
```

Fig. 3.6 - Carpark control in Concurrent Euclid.

languages.

Like CE, the basic unit of global program structure is the **module**, which encapsulates data and procedures. Some modules can be declared as monitors and mutual exclusion of access to their **entry** procedures is enforced. Modules are abstract objects, like CP's type definitions, so multiple instances of the same object may be generated, they will share the same code but will have their own private data and locking mechanism.

Mesa is very flexible in its handling of processes, which can be assigned to a variable or passed as parameters. In the same way that procedure variables represent a family of types depending on their parameter and result types, process variables represent families depending only on their result types. Any Mesa procedure may be initiated as an autonomous process provided that it will deliver the correct type of result. For example, given procedure and process definitions of the form:-

```
sqr : procedure [in : integer]
returns [out : integer] =
begin
      out ← in * in                    {← means assignment}
end
```

and

```
p : process returns [out : integer]
```

it is possible to initiate the procedure as an autonomous process and retrieve the result at some later point using the **fork** and **join** operators.

```
p ← fork sqr [5];
```

causes the procedure *sqr* to be executed as an autonomous process represented by the process variable *p*. The process and the procedure are compatible types since they both deliver an integer result. The result can be retrieved by the **join** function and used in an assignment, i.e.

$i \leftarrow$ **join** $p;$

The above two statements are equivalent to the statement:-

$i \leftarrow sqr$ [5];

except that the former method allows for some concurrent computation. In terms of program execution, the creation of a Mesa process within a program is quite simple compared to the creation of a process within a multi-user operating system environment. However, it is still an expensive operation and the overheads of establishing a process are 40 times that of a simple procedure call; process creation should, therefore, be used with some restraint.

Long-term process synchronisation in Mesa is again provided by *condition* variables which allow multiple processes to *wait* for the same condition. However, the semantics of a Mesa *notify* operation are significantly different from the semantics of the corresponding *signal* operations that are provided in other languages. In other languages a specific program state is associated with a *signal* so the recipient process is required to be resumed immediately. In contrast, Mesa's *notify* operation acts only as a hint that the program might be in a particular state. The recipient process is then resumed at some later, convenient time when the monitor becomes free. The program state may have changed between the notification of the condition and the resumption of the process, so the process must check that the condition still holds before continuing, and it may have to wait again. The use of conditions should therefore take the form:-

    while not <*ok_to_continue*> **do**
        wait c
    endloop

The weakening of the pre-condition for a *signal* operation has the advantage that signals may provide additional functions. The *broadcast* mechanism acts as a *notify*, except that all the processes waiting for a condition will be resumed, not just one of them. Each awakened process can then decide whether to resume its execution or to *wait* in the condition again.

The weakened condition means that a *timeout* may be associated with a *condition* so that all processes will be periodically restarted and given the opportunity to take some alternative action.

Mesa probably represents the most sophisticated development of the monitor concept and provides a very dynamic environment. This does, however, bring the attendant problems of illegal references etc. These are in part compensated for by the inclusion of exception handling routines, but their provision, implementation and use in a concurrent environment can prove difficult.

3.3.3. Modula and Modula-2

Modula was designed by Niklaus Wirth at ETH Zurich in 1975 (1977a) with the aim of providing a very small, efficient language for programming industrial control and real-time systems. It was intended to run on a 'bare machine' without any operating system support. By careful design and 'tuning' the language towards the target architecture of the PDP-11 family of computers, it was possible to implement the language with a kernel consisting of only 300 bytes of assembly code, as opposed to CP's 12k bytes. This tiny memory requirement, as well as the language's elegance, has led to its growing importance.

Modula is heavily influenced by Pascal and retains much of the that language's structure, to which modules with import and export clauses are added. Processes are explicitly provided together with monitors which are called **interface modules**. Unfortunately, these constructs are not parametrised and cannot be replicated. The language prohibits nested monitor calls.

Process synchronisation is provided by *wait* and *send* operations on *signal* variables, which are implemented as queues of waiting processes that can be sorted by priority. The simplicity of Modula's implementation may be attributed to the fact that the *only* points in a program at which the processor may change its context are these *wait* and *send* operations. Modula does not provide the time-slicing mechanisms that form part of the implementation of most other concurrent programming languages. This means that the operations of context saving and restoring are greatly simplified and are partly handled by the compiler. The scheduling algorithms and housekeeping functions are also kept at a minimum. Furthermore, there is no need for a monitor 'gate' or locking mechanism since all processes, other than the active process, are known to be suspended at a *wait* or a *send* operation. An unfortunate consequence of this approach is that the programmer needs to be aware of the scheduling policy when designing a program, and must include frequent *signal* operations to ensure the smooth concurrent progress of a program.

The design of Modula underwent a major revision between 1977 and 1980 to re-emerge as Modula-2 (Wirth, 1983) (sometimes confusingly referred to simply as Modula). During the revision, the direct implementation of process and monitor constructs were removed from the language, leaving only modules and procedures. The features for concurrency can be re-introduced using standard modules to implement process creation, swapping and synchronisation. This approach has two major disadvantages.

(1)   Since the features are no longer part of the language the compiler cannot provide as much semantic checking on their use.

(2)   Although a set of features is defined in Wirth's book, this does not constitute a standard definition, and some implementations provide different facilities. This position is likely to improve after the introduction of the proposed BSI standard.

The wide availability of Modula-2 on several popular machines and its elegant structure means that it is an important sequential language as well as a concurrent one.

3.4. SUMMARY

This chapter has examined the use of monitors as a basis for implementing concurrent systems. The semantics of monitors are very close to many problem domains which involve shared data and, consequently, provide some very elegant solutions.

Monitor-based systems are essentially asynchronous, consisting of groups of autonomous processes. Monitors are expected to provide only short-term synchronisation to ensure the integrity of shared data. The longer term synchronisation and resource allocation strategies require some additional features. Hoare (1972), first proposed that the programmer should specify named *conditions* consisting of a boolean expression involving the monitor's variables. A process could then wait for a particular *condition* to be satisfied, e.g.

> *non_full :* **condition** *:= (spaces < max_spaces);*
>
> ...
>
> *wait (non-full)*

This method assumed that the compiler would generate code to evaluate periodically the *conditions* defined within the program and to restart any eligible processes. · In practice, most implementations have provided a more direct mechanism by which processes directly synchronise their operation, so the programmer must provide the code to evaluate conditions and to restart processes.

Monitor-based systems have been very successful and have been widely used. However, they do impose some constraints and limitations on the structure of programs. For these reasons, research to develop concurrent languages has shifted to the development of the paradigms discussed in the following chapters.

4

Message Based
Interaction

4.1. INTRODUCTION

Many operating systems have used the concept of message exchange to provide the basic means of communication and synchronisation between processes. Recently the concept has been incorporated into the design of programming languages. Message systems remove all responsibility for the management of shared memory from the programmer and subsume it in the implementation of the support software. Instead of the shared 'address-space' of the monitor based approach, the programmer is provided with a shared 'name-space' and the facility to exchange messages between named objects.

In many cases the actual implementation of the message system may employ shared memory areas and monitors; message passing, therefore, is not a primitive mechanism. However, the method does have the advantage that it makes fewer assumptions about the underlying hardware, since shared memory is not required, so message systems can easily be implemented on a network of processors connected by a communications system.

Access to the message facility is usually implemented by calls to operating system routines. The message routines can be incorporated into a standard high-level language, such as Fortran or Pascal, which is then used to implement the application's processes as independent programs. This approach is popular as an inexpensive method of providing concurrent systems, since existing compilers can be used. More recently languages have been developed which directly incorporate the concept of message passing between processes.

In most implementations, message-passing is treated as analogous to the input/output operations which are provided for communication with the filing system or peripheral devices. All message systems provide at least two basic operations of the general form:-

> **send** *<message>* { **to** *<destination>*}

and

> **receive** *<message>* {**from** *<source>*} {**about** *<subject>*}

(where optional fields are enclosed in braces {}).

The semantics of these two operations can vary considerably, depending on:-

> The patterns of communications supported.
> Details of the naming conventions.
> The form of the message.
> The possible selection criteria for receipt.
> Synchronisation constraints.

Many of these aspects are mutually independent, which means that there is a wide range of possible implementations, many of which have been developed. Of these features, the synchronisation constraint imposed upon the communication has the greatest impact upon the structure of programs. The later sections of this chapter demonstrate the effects of adopting different policies on this aspect by examining the use of two contrasting programming languages, PLITS and CSP, which respectively implement asynchronous and synchronous message exchange.

4.1.1. Communications patterns and naming

Communication by message exchange requires the active co-operation of both parties. The originator of the message must invoke a **send** operation and supply the message as a parameter. The recipient must invoke a **receive** operation, supplying the name or memory address of some local variable as the destination of the message.

Four patterns of communication can be distinguished, according to how a process specifies the destination of a message that it is sending, and on how a process specifies the source of the next message that it is willing to receive. The patterns are:-

One to one:

> where both parties to the exchange specify the other as the only possible partner to the communication.

N to one:

> where a process is prepared to accept a message from any one of a set of processes, and the sending process specifies the destination process. Typically this pattern is used by a utility process which provides a service for a number of customer processes.

One to N:

> where a process can 'broadcast' a message to be received by a number of processes. In this case the same message may be acted upon by more than one of the destination processes. Broadcasts are used to disseminate status information around a system, or to solicit information from an unknown source.

M to N:

> the generalised broadcast with a number of senders.

The communication patterns that are available depend on the way in which the names of processes are disseminated throughout the system, and on the way in which they can be specified as parameters to the **send** and **receive** operations. Some systems can support a selection of patterns, others only provide one.

For the programmer, the implementation of a particular application is greatly simplified if a concurrent language is available which allows the component processes to be specified in a single program. This allows the partner to a communication to be specified using the identifier given with its definition within the program. The mapping from program identifiers to operating system process-identifiers or memory addresses can then be performed by the support software.

The situation is more complex when the processes are specified as independent programs which are linked together at a later stage. In some cases this is performed by a linkage-editor at the same time as the calls to library functions are resolved; in this case the program identifiers that are used in the component programs are correlated and checked. Some errors which would normally be detected by the compiler of a concurrent language, such as references to non-existent processes, may be detected at this stage, but in general, the degree of checking and the quality of diagnostic messages tend to be inferior.

The situation is more complicated if the linking is not performed until the programs are actually executed. In this case, the operating system must provide some form of 'name-keeper' service to bind program names to entities in the executing environment. Where the execution environment consists of a number of processors connected by a 'local area network' (LAN), the name-keeping service requires the continuous cooperation of support protocols in each processor to maintain information concerning the current system status.

The problems of name resolution can be alleviated by introducing some intermediate system object between processes. These intermediaries have been given a variety of names, such as ports, mailboxes, gates and sockets; where each facility has subtly different semantics. Here they will be referred to generically as ports. All these mechanisms provide the equivalent of pointer or reference variables for processes, which are initialised by the operating system. Processes send their messages to named ports. The

operating system then performs some degree of message buffering, initiates
any necessary transmission over the LAN, and finally delivers the message to
a process ready to receive a message from the given port name. This
removes the necessity for a process to be aware of the exact identity of its
correspondent. One party may even change without the other being aware of
the fact.

4.1.2. Message form

The methodology used in the production of a program determines the flexibility and safety of message formation and interpretation. If the entire software
system is compiled as a single unit, or if extensive support is given to checking program interfaces, the type checking of message systems can be as
comprehensive as that of procedure based languages. The form of the message can be defined as a structured type similar to a record and the compiler
can enforce the correct interpretation of the fields.

Without adequate linguistic support for the structuring and interpretation of messages, the programmer is provided merely with a mechanism for
passing strings of bytes between processes. The correct construction and
interpretation of the messages is dependent on the programmer defining and
implementing suitable protocols within each process. The situation may be
further complicated if the message system implements messages only of some
fixed size, meaning that a logical message either be padded to the required
size or be fragmented into a series of physical messages or 'packets'.

Sometimes, the passing of messages between processes residing on a
machine with common memory can be optimised by simply passing a reference to the message (i.e. its memory address). However, if the hardware
architecture is oriented towards enhanced process protection by the use of disjoint address spaces, it may be necessary to copy contents of the message
between process environments within the same machine. If the message system is implemented in a distributed environment the form of the facilities
provided will be restricted by the underlying environment provided by the
network protocols.

4.1.3. Sequencing and synchronisation

Some systems allow processes some control over the order in which they
accept messages. One simple way to implement such choice is to provide the
process with access to a number of 'ports'. The programmer then assigns
logical functions to each port, so that the receiving process can choose which
class of message to service next. To allow adequate flexibility, processes
must be able to determine whether there are any pending messages on a port
before initiating a receive operation, or to abort a **receive** operation if no
messages are available.

In general, messages are received by a process in the order in which
they are sent. However, some systems provide priorities for messages so that

important messages pass through the network faster and 'jump the queue' at the recipient's end. Priority messages are usually found in control systems to implement alarms and emergency routines, and in large networks to implement network management functions.

More sophisticated, language-based message systems can provide more comprehensive control of receipt based on the content of the messages. This is made possible by having the structure of the messages formally defined in the program. For example, PLITS messages may contain a 'transaction key' and a process may indicate that it wishes to receive messages only with a particular key.

The final variation between systems is their degree of synchronisation between the parties to an exchange. The more common option is that of asynchronous exchange. The originator of a message initiates a **send** operation which is immediately executed. The message is accepted by the underlying implementation and eventually delivered to its destination process. A process wishing to receive a message will be delayed until a suitable message is available, although in practice some means of avoiding the delay is also necessary. A disadvantage of asynchronous systems their need for extensive support in their implementation to provide for the buffering of unreceived messages. In principle the buffering requirements are unlimited. In practice a sending process may become delayed waiting for a buffer, or messages may be arbitrarily discarded when buffer space is exhausted.

Another drawback of asynchronous systems is that the sender does not know when, or if, a message is received, so it cannot make any assumption concerning the status of its partner to the communication. If an acknowledgement is required, the recipient must explicitly send a reply message.

The alternative is synchronous message passing. Under this regime the sender, as well as the receiver of a message, may become delayed until the partner is ready. The message exchange then proceeds and both processes are simultaneously resumed. Synchronous systems have the advantage that only limited message buffering is required, and some aspects of programming are simplified since knowledge of the status of other processes is more directly available. The disadvantages lie in the difficulty of implementing the synchronism, especially if the substratum of the message implementation is based on asynchronous principles. Synchronous systems are considered in more detail in section 4.3 where the synchronous language CSP is examined.

4.1.4. Structure of programs

The different nature of the coordination facilities provided by monitor based or message based systems leads to superficially different structures of programs.

Simple communication between processes can be quite cumbersome in a monitor based system, and it requires the programmer to define a communication channel explicitly in the form of a buffer monitor. This facility is often provided as a primitive of a message system.

Coordination between processes is provided by exclusive access to shared monitor variables. Message systems do not provide shared variables, they are all private; the control of a shared resource is implemented by a separate process which contains the variables. Instead of calling a monitor procedure, processes send a message to the resource-manager process requesting that an operation be performed. The client then waits for a reply from the manager acknowledging that the operation has been performed and returning any results. The 'mutual exclusion' is provided by the fact that the variables can be accessed only by the manager, which services one message request at a time.

The longer term synchronisation of access to resources, which is implemented by conditions or queues in monitors, can be provided in message systems by the selective receipt of messages. A manager simply refuses to service requests for a service once its resources are exhausted, so the client processes are delayed waiting for the manager's reply.

Just as monitors should be able to use the services of other monitors, service processes should be able to call upon other service processes in a nested manner. Again careful program structuring is needed to avoid deadlock. The next sections will examine the programming techniques in more detail.

4.2. ASYNCHRONOUS MESSAGE PASSING - PLITS

There have been very few serious attempts to integrate the concepts of asynchronous message passing into the framework of a high-level language. The most widely known is PLITS (Programming Language In The Sky) developed at the University of Rochester by a team led by J. Feldman (1979). The PLITS project examined several aspects of programming language design and development, but only the treatment of concurrency will be considered here. PLITS refines message passing into a series of operations which can be amalgamated with other languages to give a concurrent environment. This section will follow Feldman and present "Pascal-PLITS" although in theory a program could be composed of a series of modules written in a combination of languages.

4.2.1. Modules

A PLITS program consists of a series of autonomous modules which implement the processes. The internal structure of a module corresponds to a Pascal program. A module is introduced as a new structured object (c.f. processes in CP). The keyword **mod** is used to introduce a definition, with the form:-

```
type T = mod <parameter_list>;
      begin
              <body>
      end
```

Casting the module definition as a type definition allows several instances to be generated and the *<parameter_list>* allows the definitions to be passed different initial conditions through simple value parameters.

Modules can be created dynamically within a program, at which point they are allocated a unique system-generated name (c.f. process-id). PLITS introduces a new type of primitive variable, the *module*, to store or manipulate these names. *module* variables are somewhat analogous to pointer variables since they are used to refer to other objects. However, their type-compatibility is broader and can be used to refer to *any* type of module; i.e. they can refer to any object that is created from a definition that begins with the keyword **mod**. This is analogous to having a variable which can refer to any sort of record. However, the operations on module variables are very restricted so this facility does not significantly weaken the security of the language. A module variable can be used in an assignment-like statement to generate a new instance of a module from a type-definition (c.f. Mesa's **fork** operation), i.e.

```
type T = mod i : integer;
      begin
              <body>
      end;

var
      V : module;

      ...
      V := T(5)
      ...
```

This creates a new, autonomous module of type *T* with an initial value of 5 for its local integer *i*. The value of *V* is set to the name of this new module.

Once a module has been created it continues independently of its 'parent', and disappears only by executing a **self-destruct** statement. A module can determine whether a particular named module still exists by calling the built-in **extant** function which returns a boolean value. This is the limit to the information that a module can obtain about another without its active, programmed co-operation.

PLITS programs often require a single instance of a module that provides a service for several other modules, each of which needs to know the name of the server. PLITS simplifies the establishment of such program structures by by allowing modules to be defined in a constant definition, i.e.

const

> *server* = **mod**
> > **begin**
> > > *<body>*
> > **end**

This defines and generates a single instance of the *server*. It cannot be used to generate other instances and therefore cannot be parametrised. Since its name is unique, and known to the compiler, the module can be referenced directly by other modules using the constant name (e.g. *server*) rather than by using an initialised *module* variable.

4.2.2. Messages

Inter-module communication is effected by message exchange which is implemented by the support software. A message is composed of a set of name-value pairs or *slots*. The type of value that can be assigned to each slot must be declared, and must be a primitive type (integer, character etc.), a *module* (to pass module names around), or a **transaction** (a new basic type discussed later in this section).

Each module definition includes a **public** section in which the names and types of all message slots known within the module must be declared. The union of all these definitions identifies the total set of message slots. The compiler can check that modules of a program are consistent in their interpretation of common slots.

Modules may declare local variables of type **message** to store or manipulate messages that either have been received from other modules, or are destined to be sent to other modules. All messages have the potential to contain all slots, but a module can access only those slots that it has declared as public. Thus a module can be used as an intermediary, forwarding messages between other modules but not needing to be aware of the form or content of the message. This provides a useful degree of modularity of program structure.

Message variables can be treated similarly to **record** structures. Individual slots can be accessed using the usual dot notation (i.e. *<message_name>.<slot_name>*), or complete messages can be copied by an assignment statement. Although all messages have the potential to contain all slots, in practice they contain only a subset. The initial selection of slots that are present in a message is determined when the message is created, using a message-composition statement of the form:-

mess1 := **message**
> (
> *<slot_name_1>* ˜ *<value_1>*,
> *<slot_name_2>* ˜ *<value_2>*
>)

Additional slots can be included using a statement of the form:-

put *<slot_name_4>* ˜ *<value_4>* **in** *mess_1*

Slots can be removed as follows:-

remove *<slot_name_1>* **from** *mess_1*

An attempt to access the value of a slot that is not present in a message causes an execution error. The programmer can guard against this possibility using the two language constructs, **present** and **absent**, which return a boolean value indicating the status of a slot within a particular message.

Having composed its message, a module can send it to another named module using a statement of the form:-

send *<message>* **to** *<destination>*

The underlying implementation then takes a copy of the message and the module continues its execution. Once the message has been sent, the originator has no control over its progress towards its destination, nor can it gain any information about the status of the message.

The message will be delivered when the designated recipient executes a statement of the form:-

receive *<message>*

or

receive *<message>* **from** *<originator>*

At this point the contents of the message are copied into the specified local variable (*<message>*) and the version belonging to the underlying implementation is discarded. The recipient can then manipulate the known message slots (i.e. those it has declared as **public**).

A module can specify that it only wishes to receive messages from a particular module, or it may accept any message destined for it. If no appropriate messages are available the module will be delayed until one is. A module can avoid becoming delayed by using the **pending** function to check whether there are any suitable messages before executing a **receive** operation.

PLITS provides a new primitive type of variable, the *transaction*, which can be used with **send**, **recieve** and **pending** operations to establish flexible communication patterns. Values of type *transaction* are produced by the function **new-transaction**, which delivers a series of unique values that can be stored in *transaction* variables. Messages automatically incorporate a *transaction* slot which can hold a transaction value. The values stored in this slot is set by including an 'about' clause in a **send** operation. For example,

send *<message>* **to** *fireservice* **about** *emergency*

The **pending** and **receive** operations can also include an 'about' clause to confine their operation to messages with a specific value in the *transaction* slot. For example, the *fireservice* module can give priority to incoming emergency messages using the following statement:-

if pending about *emergency*
      then
                      receive *message* **about** *emergency*
      else
                      receive *message*

4.2.3. Example PLITS programs

Implementing the data-logger example described in section 2.2 using PLITS is trivially simple. The conceptualisation of the logger as three asynchronous processes communicating by messages is precisely the same as the underlying PLITS model, so the basic requirements are met by the underlying implementation. Since only one example of each of the three forms of module is required they can be specified in constant definitions and simply named in the **send** and **receive** operations. The outline of the program is given in Fig. 4.1.

The *inputter* module simply samples the input data at the appropriate time and composes it into a message to send to the *calculator*. The *calculator* accumulates the values from these messages, when enough samples have arrived it calculates their mean values and standard deviations which it assembles into a message variable and sends to the *storer* module. During the calculation phase it may be necessary for the implementation to buffer the messages that are generated by the *inputter* and then deliver them later, in the correct sequence. The *storer* also buffers data from messages which it then stores on disk. Note that all messages potentially have three slots, but in practice only two forms of messages are used. PLITS gives a simple clean design; its limitations will depend on the quality and efficiency of the underlying message implementation and on its buffering capacity.

The carpark controller also requires three types of module: a resource administrator, *space_control*, which provides the overall coordination; and two types of processes, *entrance_control* and *exit_control*, to control the gates. The latter types can be conveniently defined as parametrised type definitions which are initialised to identify which gate they control. The structure is illustrated in Fig. 4.2.

The *exit_control* module simply monitors the departure of cars and informs *space_control* by sending a null message. The message needs to include only a transaction field to enable *space_control* to be selective about the class of message it receives when the carpark is full. It can be programmed as:-

type *exit_control* = **mod** *gateno : integer; class : transaction;*

begin
        while *<carpark_open>* **do**
           begin
                <await_customer_at gateno>;
                send message *()* **to** *space_control* **about** *class;*
                <dismiss_customer>;
           end *{while}*
    end; *{exit_control}*

The *entrance_control* is similar except that it needs to wait for a response from *space_control* acknowledging that a space has been allocated to it. The message therefore needs a *module* field identifying the sender in order that the reply can be routed back. (Alternatively a second *transaction* field can be uniquely initialised for each *entrance_control* process).

type *entrance_control* = **mod** *gateno : integer; class : transaction;*
begin
        public
           sender : module;

        var
           m : message;

        ...
        while *<carpark_open>* **do**
           begin
                <await_customer_at gateno>;

                send message *(sender ˉ me)* **to** *space_control*
                                    about *class;*
                receive *m;*

                <admit_customer>
           end *{while}*

    ...
    end *{entrance_control}*

When the carpark is full *space_control* accepts messages only from the *exit_control*s. This means that the *entrance_control*s may be delayed waiting for a reply message until room is available. To allow this selective waiting, *space_control* uses two *transaction* variables *arrival* and *departure*, these must be initialised to the values which are passed as parameters to the *entrance_control* and *exit_control* modules.

```
const inputter = mod;
begin
        public
                raw : integer;
        ...
        while <system_running> do
                begin
                        <input_data>;
                        send message (raw ~ data) to calculator
                end;
        ...
end {of inputter}


const calculator = mod;
begin
        public
                raw             : integer;
                mean, sd        : real;

        var
                buf : array[1..size] of integer;
                messin, messout  : message;
                lmean, lsd       : real;

        ...
        while <system_running> do
                begin
                        for i := 1 to size do
                                begin
                                        receive messin from inputter;
                                        buf[i] := messin.raw
                                end;

                        <calculate lmean and lsd>;

                        messout.mean    := lmean;
                        messout.sd      := lsd;
                        send messout to storer;
                end; {while}
        ...
end; {of calculator}


const storer = mod;
begin
```

```
public
        mean, sd : real;
var
        buffer_1, buffer_2 : array[1..size] of real;
        messin : message;
...
while <system_running> do
        begin
                for i := 1 to size do
                        begin
                                receive messin from calculator;
                                buffer_1[i] := messin.mean;
                                buffer_2[i] := messin.sd
                        end;
                <store_block_data>;
        end; {while}
...
end; {Storer}
```

Fig. 4.1 - Data logger in PLITS.

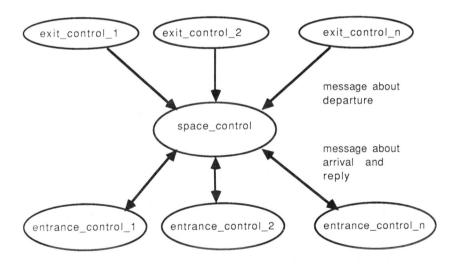

Fig. 4.2 - Structure of a simple carpark controller.

```
const space_control = mod;
begin
        public
                sender : module;

        var
                spaces   : integer;
                m        : message;

                arrival, departure : transaction;
                {initialised to same values as class in
                entrance_control and exit_control respectively}

        ...
        spaces := max_spaces;
        while <carpark_open> do
                if spaces = 0 then
                        begin
                                receive m about departure;
                                spaces := spaces + 1
                        end
                else
                        begin
                                receive m;
                                if m.about = departure then
                                        spaces := spaces + 1
                                else
                                        begin
                                        spaces := spaces - 1;
                                        send message () to m.sender;
                                        end
                        end
        end; {while}
        ...
end {space_control}
```

This solution suffers from the same problem as the previous solutions that used semaphores and monitors, since an *entrance_control* process may be subjected to an indeterminate delay when the carpark is full. The problem can be overcome by using the 'nested' module structure illustrated in Fig. 4.3; the revised program structure is outlined in Fig. 4.4. With this structure, *space_control* accepts all messages and replies immediately. The reply may indicate that a space has been allocated, in which case the customer can be admitted. Alternatively, the reply may be that there is no room, in which case the customer is informed that there is likely to be a delay. The *entrance_control* then waits for a second message informing it that it can proceed.

space_control passes all the outstanding requests for spaces to the *queuer* module, which maintains a queue of waiting requests in its input message queue. When space becomes available, *space_control* informs *queuer*, which informs the first waiting *entrance_control*. The operation of *exit_control* is unaffected by these changes.

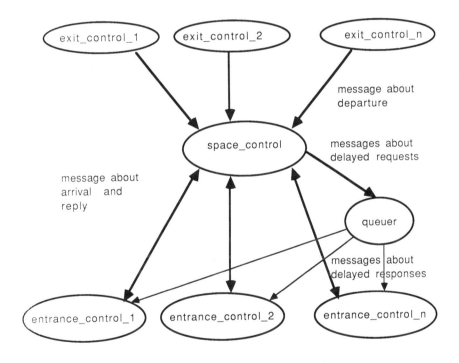

Fig. 4.3 - Carpark control with nested structure.

type *exit_control* = **mod** *gateno : integer; class : transaction;*
[as previous example]

type *entrance_control* = **mod** *gateno : integer; class : transaction;*
begin
        public
                sender   : module;
                full   : boolean;
        var
                m : message;
        ...
        while *<carpark_open>* **do**
                begin
                        <await_customer_at gateno>;
                        send message *(sender ⁻ me)* **to** *space_control*
                                      about *class;*
                        receive *m;*
                        if *m.full* **then**
                                begin
                                        <indicate_delay>;
                                        receive *m;*
                                        <rescind_delay>
                            end;
                        <admit_customer>
                end; *{while}*
                ...
end; *{entrance_control}*

const *space_control* = **mod;**
begin
        public
                sender   : module;
                full   : boolean;
        var
                m : message;
                spaces, waiting : integer;
                arrival, departure : transaction;

        ...
        spaces   := max_spaces;
        waiting := 0;
        while *<carpark_open>* **do**
        begin
                receive *m;*

```
                    if m.about = departure then
                        if waiting > O then
                                begin
                                        send message () to queuer
                                                about departure;
                                        waiting := waiting - 1;
                                end
                        else
                                spaces := spaces + 1

                    else {about=arrival}
                        if spaces > O then
                                begin {no problem}
                                spaces := spaces - 1;
                                send message (full ¯ false)
                                                to m.sender
                                end
                        else
                                begin {queue request}
                                send message (full ¯ true)
                                                to m.sender;
                                waiting := waiting + 1;
                                send m to queuer about arrival;
                                end

            end; {while}
            ...
end {space_control};

const queuer = mod;
begin
        public
                sender : module;
        var
                m : message;
        ...
        while <carpark_open> do
                begin
                        receive m about departure;
                        receive m about arrival;
                        send message () to m.sender
                end;
        ...
end; {queuer}
```

Fig. 4.4 - Outline program of revised carpark controller.

4.2.4. Summary of PLITS

PLITS provides an extensive set of flexible facilities resulting in a rich, powerful and dynamic programming environment. Both n-to-one and one-to-one communication patterns are supported, but not broadcasts, since the sender of a message must specify its destination. This allows the implementation easily to identify the destination of each message, and simplifies its routing and queuing.

The manipulation of module names is very flexible, and they can be disseminated throughout the system and stored in program variables. This is essential in order to support the dynamic creation of autonomous modules and allows sophisticated communications patterns to be established.

Messages take the form of named slots of particular data types. This provides the same level of security through type-checking as that provided by the parameter mechanisms in procedure-based techniques, since the compiler can ensure the uniform reference to message slots across the modules. The system has an added advantage for information-hiding since some slots in a message may be inaccessible to the module handling it. A disadvantage of the scheme is that all messages have the same form which can lead to inefficiencies in implementation; some partitioning of the forms of messages and the introduction of some mechanism that controls the visibility of slot names is desirable. It would be useful to relax the constraint that slots can only be of primitive types to simplify the inclusion of structured types in messages.

Modules have considerable flexibility in controlling the receipt of messages and they may elect to receive any message or only to receive those from a specified module, or, by the use of transaction variables, may select messages concerning a particular subject. This flexibility is further enhanced by the ability to inspect the queue of waiting messages through the use of the pending function. This facility is necessary since a module may become blocked on a receive operation if there are no suitable messages outstanding. A useful extension would be to allow the specification of sets of modules or transactions in a receive operation; for instance, it would have simplified the carpark example's *space_control* module if it could have specified the "set of all *exit_controls*" rather than having to use a transaction variable.

PLITS is essentially asynchronous; in theory, a module is unlimited in its total output or rate of message production. In practice, the pool of message buffers is limited, so a module may be delayed on a send operation if the pool becomes exhausted. However, this would probably be symptomatic of some serious fault in the program's design or operation. PLITS provides an interesting, flexible programming environment. It is unfortunate that it is not more readily available.

4.3. SYNCHRONOUS MESSAGE PASSING - CSP

Communicating Sequential Processes (CSP) was proposed as a preliminary solution to the problem of defining a synchronous message-based language (Hoare, 1978). It was not intended to be used as a programming language *per se*, but reflects Hoare's concerns of proving the correctness of programs. It has a very terse, mathematical style of notation rather than the English-like reserved words and constructs of languages designed for programming, such as Pascal. However, CSP provided a medium for the discussion of synchronous systems and has inspired a great deal of development. Since the original paper Hoare has refined his ideas slightly and some changes can be found in his book, (Hoare, 1985). However, the original version is the most widely cited and will be discussed here. CSP has been widely criticised for its unique notation which introduces an initial overhead for the casual reader. Most of the concepts, however, have already been introduced in previous sections of this book so the transition should not be too difficult.

CSP uses square brackets ([,]) to delineate the start and end of most language constructs, for example, in place of **begin** and **end** in compound statements. All conditional or repetitive execution is provided by Dijkstra's 'guarded commands' (introduced in section 1.2.4.1) using a modified notation. The **if**, **fi** delineators are again replaced by square brackets while the separator □ is retained. 'Alternative' constructs therefore have the form :-

$$
\begin{array}{l}
[\\
\quad\quad <guard> \rightarrow \quad <guarded\_list> \\
\square \\
\quad\quad <guard> \rightarrow \quad <guarded\_list> \\
\quad\quad ... \\
]
\end{array}
$$

All of the guards are evaluated and one of those that evaluates to **true** is selected and its corresponding *<guarded_list>* is executed. The repetitive construct is introduced by the symbol *[rather than **do**, e.g.

$$
\begin{array}{l}
*[\\
\quad\quad i > 0 \rightarrow i := i - 1 \\
\square \\
\quad\quad j > 0 \rightarrow j := j - 1 \\
]
\end{array}
$$

The command is repeatedly executed until no guard evaluates to true, i.e. until both i and j in the example are zero or negative.

A CSP program consists of a static collection of processes. A process is usually identified by a name prefixed to its definition. The structure of the program is defined in a *<parallel_command>* which introduces the processes. A CSP convention allows capitalised words to be used as abbreviations for program text defined separately. The structure of the data-logger can therefore be defined by the statement:-

```
[
  inputter            :: INPUTTER
  calculator          :: CALCULATOR
  storer              :: STORER
]
```

This introduces the three processes but defers the detailed definition of variable declarations and statements. The usual range of primitive types are allowed, and these may be composed into arrays or structures. All variables are static, but they may be declared anywhere in a program and exist for the duration of the enclosing block. There are no pointers or dynamic variables. All variables are private to their enclosing process definitions, which means that programs consist of a series of disjoint address spaces.

Arrays are of fixed length whose bounds must be given on declaration; they are subscripted in the usual manner. Parentheses, (), rather than square brackets,[ ], are used to enclose the subscripts, e.g.

buf : (1..max) integer;

buf(i) := val

Structures are not declared as types, as they are in Pascal, nor are individual fields selectable in the usual manner. Structures are composed or decomposed in assignment statements using named 'constructors'. A particular constructor always takes the same number of parameters, each always of the same type. Parameters to constructors are enclosed in parentheses. The constructor forms a new structured object from its parameters. Used on the right-hand-side of an assignment statement, it produces a structured value which can be assigned to a suitable variable. For example, the statement

x := cons (first, second)

constructs a structured value consisting of two components and assigns the result to the variable *x*. When used on the left-hand-side of an assignment, a constructor temporarily composes a suitable selection of variables into a structure so that the individual components can be assigned the values from the corresponding fields of a structure that has been produced by the operation of the same constructor. For example, the two statements

x := cons (first, second);
cons (y,z) := x

would result in the assignment of the value of *first* to *y* and the value of *second* to *z*. Constructors generate unique forms of structured types; structures with the same components which have been generated using different constructors are not compatible. For example, the assignment

cons2 (a, b) := cons (y, z)

would fail because of incompatible structures. Unfortunately, the use of parentheses for both array subscripting and structure construction can sometimes lead to confusion when interpreting programs because the same textual form represents different operations.

4.3.1. Process interaction

Coordination between processes is implemented by message exchange between pairs of processes. It involves the synchronised execution of **send** and **receive** operations by both processes, each process must explicitly name the other. The message can be the value of any variable or structured type, provided that the source values and target variables are compatible. If these conditions are met, the operations are said to 'match', the values are assigned to the target variables, and the processes then resume their independent execution. **send** and **receive** statements take the forms:-

> *<destination_process_name> ! <expression>*

and

> *<source_process_name> ? <target_variable>*

For example, the execution of the two processes:-

> *inputter::*   *calculator::*
> ...   ...
> *calculator ! val*   *inputter ? buf(i)*
> ...   ...

would result in the value of *val* being assigned to *buf(i)*. Communication is strictly synchronous and either party may be delayed at the message operation until its specified partner executes a matching command.

The tight, deterministic synchronisation of this organisation is inappropriate for most applications, and flexibility is provided by allowing input statements to be included in the guards of guarded commands, in combination with other boolean expressions. The evaluation of a guard containing an input command will produce one of three conditions:-

(1)   The message exchange can proceed without delay, i.e. the partner is delayed at a corresponding output command. In this case the input component of the guard evaluates to true. If the other components of the guard also evaluate to true then the guard succeeds.

(2)   The message exchange can never proceed, i.e. the partner process has terminated, and the guard fails.

(3)   The partner process still exists but it has not yet executed a corresponding command. In this case the guard neither succeeds nor fails at this point and it may have to be reevaluated later.

The evaluation of the guards of a guarded command will result in one of three situations:-

(1)   One or more guards succeed, in which case one successful guard is selected and the corresponding *<guarded_list>* is executed.

(2)   All guards fail, in which case the guarded command is terminated or aborted.

(3)   The result is not determined if some guards fall into the third category give above, and they may yet succeed. In this case execution is delayed and guards are repeatedly re-evaluated until a definite result is obtained.

The data-logger input process needs to be synchronised with the external environment and cannot wait for a synchronous message exchange with the calculator process. Therefore buffering is needed between the processes. In CSP these must take the form of extra processes using guarded commands to provide the non-determinism. The program therefore consists of five processes:-

```
[
        inputter              :: INPUTTER
        buffer_1              :: BUFFER_1
        calculator            :: CALCULATOR
        buffer_2              :: BUFFER_2
        storer                :: STORER
]
```

The program code of *buffer_1*, shown in Fig. 4.5, implements a circular buffer. The *buffer_1* either receives data from the *inputter*, which it stores internally, or the *buffer_1* receives a message from the *calculator* requesting further data, in which case the *buffer_1* sends the data in a message to the *calculator*. This asymmetry of design arises because output commands are not allowed to appear in guards. In the example, *buffer_1* and *calculator* communicate using a signal, which is a special form of structured object which has no components; only the names of the constructors need to match for synchronisation to take place. *buffer_2* will have an analogous structure, but it will have to name explicitly the other processes with which it interacts.

4.3.2. Process arrays

CSP provides multiple versions of similar processes by expanding the array concept to give arrays of processes. For example,

    [entrance_control (i : 1..max_gates) :: ENTRANCE_CONTROL]

defines an array of *max_gates* processes; individual processes are referenced using the standard array subscripting notation, i.e. *entrance_control(1)*, etc. All of the processes share the same definition, which is given elsewhere in *ENTRANCE_CONTROL*. The differences between the processes arise because a different value is substituted for the 'bound variable', *i*, in each definition, which results in a primitive parametrisation mechanism. The processes are mutually independent, and both the array name and the index value must be

INPUTTER::
    *[val : integer;
            system_running →
                    {ie while system running do}
                    <input_data_value>;   {input data}
                    buffer_1 ! val;   {send to buffer}
    ]

CALCULATOR::
    *[buf : (1..max) integer; i : integer;
            system_running →
                i := 1;

                *[
                        i <= max →   {for i:=1 to max}
                              buffer_1 ! request ();
                              buffer_1 ? lbuf(i);
                              i := i + 1
                    ]

                <calculate>;

                buffer_2 ! cons (mean, sd) {send as structure}
    ]

BUFFER_1::
    [buffer : (0..max_buf) integer;
     next_in, next_out, count : integer;

    next_in := 0;
    next_out := 0;
    count   := 0;

    *[
            count < max_buf + 1; inputter ? buffer (next_in) →

            {lst guard - room in buffer and input ready?}

                next_in := next_in + 1 **mod** (max_buf + 1)
                count := count + 1   {update pointers}
      □

count > 0; calculator ? request () →

{2nd guard - data available and requested}

calculator ! buffer (next_out)   {send data}
next_out := next_out + 1 **mod** *(max_buf + 1)*
count := count - 1   {update pointers}

] {end of guarded command}
] {end of BUFFER_1}

Fig. 4.5 - Buffer using guarded command in CSP.

specified to communicate with one, i.e.

entrance_control(1) ! val

Process arrays can be usefully combined with a similar notation which provides an array of guards and parametrised guarded lists. For example, the following program:-

doubler::

[

(i : 1..n) producer(i) ? j → consumer(i) ! 2*j

]

defines a process that implements an array of *n* guards, each waiting for communication from an array of *producer* processes. The operation of *doubler* would forward twice the value of any input message from a *producer* to the corresponding process in an array of *consumer* processes.

Fig. 4.6 gives an outline for the carpark controller using these constructs. Each gate controller is parametrised to handle a particular gate. Events are signalled to *space_control*, which uses parametrised guarded commands to wait for input from any of these processes; when it does, it updates the count *spaces*. The second guard, (*spaces > 0*), enables the acceptance of messages from *entrance_control* processes only when the carpark is not full. In contrast with the PLITS program, no acknowledgement is necessary since the *entrance_control* will be delayed automatically until room is available and the request is accepted by *space_control*.

This solution, like many previous examples, fails to inform a customer if there will be a delay. This can be avoided by always accepting input requests and responding with a message giving the carpark's status. The controller must then be programmed to note outstanding requests and despatch a subsequent message when space becomes available. The overall program structure of the carpark controller would then become very similar to the structure developed previously in this chapter using PLITS.

```
[
        entrance_control(i : 1..max_gates) :: ENTRANCE_CONTROL
        exit_control(j : 1..max_gates)       :: EXIT_CONTROL
        space_control                        :: SPACE_CONTROL
]
```

EXIT_CONTROL::
```
        *[
                carpark_open →
                        <await_leaver gate j >;
                        <dismiss_leaver gate j >
                        space_control ! departure ();

        ]
```

ENTRANCE_CONTROL::
```
        *[
                carpark_open →
                        <await-customer gate i>;
                        space_control ! request ();
                        <admit-customer gate i>

        ]
```

SPACE_CONTROL::
```
        *[
        carpark_open →
                spaces : integer;
                spaces:= max_spaces;
                *[
                        (i:1..max_gates)entrance_control(i) ? request();
                        spaces > 0
                                →

                                {entry request and room available}
                                spaces := spaces - 1
                □
                        (i:1..max_gates)exit_control(i) ? depart()
                                →

                                {exit requests always acceptable}
                                spaces := spaces + 1

                ]
        ]
```

Fig. 4.6 - Simple carpark controller.

4.3.3. Summary and evaluation of CSP

CSP gives a very clean, precise definition of processes that are driven by their inputs and synchronised by their outputs. CSP programming style involves substituting processes for many constructs, such as procedures or monitors, found in other systems.

A number of criticisms have been made of CSP, especially regarding its practical implementation. Although valid, they may be seen as unfair since they arise when trying to extend CSP beyond its initial goals.

A frequent criticism is the need to name explicitly the partner to a communication. This means that there is no simple way to include 'library processes' which provide commonly used facilities for general programming use. The difficulty arises because process definitions have to include the names of the processes that they serve. It has also been criticised for its static program structure and the inflexibility of fixed sized process arrays.

Practical difficulties arise with the implementation of input commands in guards; what appears to be a primitive operation in fact involves a multi-message dialogue (Kieburtz, 1979). A pair of processes must first establish whether the communication is possible and that they have matching commands. The destination will then select one guard and execute one input command. This means that an acknowledgement must be sent to the successful party to confirm the communication.

A number of writers have suggested that output commands, in addition to input commands, should be permitted in guards. The removal of this asymmetry in the language would simplify the programming of some common constructs; for example, the *BUFFER_1* process of Fig. 4.5 could include an output command to the *CALCULATOR* process directly in a guard, which would eliminate the need for the request message. Unfortunately, the implementation overheads are considerable when both of the commands that are relevant to a particular message exchange are included in guards. In such cases neither party will commit itself to waiting indefinitely for a particular communication, and either party may withdraw its offer of communication and select a different guard instead. A deeper analysis of the problem and a proposed solution can be found in a paper by Buckley and Silberschatz (1983).

4.4. SUMMARY

This chapter has examined some of the techniques that implement process coordination by message exchange. There are a wide range of options open to the designer of a message facility, and consequently a wide spectrum of designs have appeared in various operating systems. A major weakness of many message schemes is the lack of programming language support to enforce the consistent interpretation of messages. This problem has been addressed in language based systems such as PLITS and CSP.

5

Operation Oriented Programs

5.1. INTRODUCTION

Tony Hoare and Per Brinch Hansen established themselves as two of the most influential workers in the field of concurrent programming with their introduction of the monitor concept, which was discussed in Chapter 3. With the growth in microprocessor technology in the late 1970s, many researchers began to consider implementing systems as networks of processors. They argued that the monitor concept was an inappropriate model for such applications, since it is founded upon the concept of a centralised shared memory, and a search for software techniques that are more appropriate for distributed systems began. One of these proposals was the language CSP, in which Hoare suggested that each processor should implement only one process and that process interaction should be implemented by the synchronous exchange of messages; CSP was discussed in the preceding chapter.

Brinch Hansen's proposal was 'Distributed Processes', (DP) (Brinch Hansen, 1978). It integrates the role of monitors with the operation of processes and it introduces the concept of the 'Remote Procedure Call' (RPC) in which one process executes a procedure call on behalf of another. Process coordination in DP is essentially asynchronous, as it is in DP's predecessor CP; DP is examined in more detail in the next section.

During the same period as these developments were occuring, the United States Department of Defense (DoD) decided to take action on its software crisis. The DoD is a major consumer of software in the form of embedded command and control software in its weapons systems. These are concurrent real-time programs often running on multi-processors and usually written in assembly code. By 1974 the problems of maintenance and integration of these systems had become unmanageable, so the DoD decided that in future all of its programs would be written in one language. No existing language provided all the requirements identified by the DoD, so a 'competition' to design one was launched. The result was Ada† (DoD, 1983). Ada's principal process-coordination mechanism is the 'rendezvous' which integrates DP's remote procedure calls with CSP's synchronous communication. These aspects of Ada's design are examined in more detail in the second section of the chapter.

5.2. DISTRIBUTED PROCESSES

DP is the direct successor to CP (Concurrent Pascal) which it attempts to simplify by expanding the concept of a process to subsume the functions of monitors and classes. This results in a cleaner language definition with fewer restrictions and special cases to be considered. However, DP is more than simply a refinement of CP; the introduction of guarded commands and the use of a different co-ordination strategy leads to a change of program style.

DP is oriented to real-time systems and is, therefore, a static language with no dynamically allocated variables or heap, no recursive procedures, and no dynamic process creation. The design is focussed on a distributed implementation so there are no shared data structures; all variables are private and a process can access only its local variables directly. Process co-ordination is provided by 'common procedures' within a process which may be accessed by 'external requests' from other processes in a similar manner to the use of a monitor's entry procedures.

The general structure of DP follows Pascal with each process definition resembling a program:-

process *<name>*
<own variables>
<common procedures>
<initial_statement>

When a program starts, each process executes its *<initial_statement>* which may call local procedures or make external requests to other processes. Even if the *<initial_statement>* terminates, the process still exists and continues to service external requests from other processes. Some processes may continue their execution indefinitely, monitoring and responding to the external environment.

A remote procedure call is invoked by the symbol **call**; as in CP, both the target process and the procedure must be named, and suitable parameters must be supplied, i.e.

---

† Ada is a registered trade mark of the US Government (Ada Joint Program Office)

call *<process name>.<procedure name> (<parameters>)*

In DP processes are defined as variables, not as types. They do not have the parametrised access-rights of CP, which means that the destination for a remote operation can identified using just its name.

The parameter passing mechanisms for procedures are restricted in order to accommodate the fact that processes may reside on separate machines. Parameters are designated as either input or output. The actual input parameters are evaluated and values assigned to the formal parameters before an external request is executed. On completion of the procedure, the values of the output parameters are copied back to the variables in the calling process. There are no variable or reference parameters. Input parameters precede the output parameters in the formal parameter section of a procedure definition; the two groups are separated by a hash sign (#). The parameter section of a procedure with only output parameters will begin with a hash sign, e.g.

proc *transform (incoming : int # outgoing : int);*

or

proc *deliver (# newval : int);*

The underlying scheduling mechanisms ensure that only one operation (i.e. external request or initial statement) is active within a process at any given time. An operation proceeds without interruption until it completes its execution or becomes blocked waiting for some action by another operation within the process. Control then passes to another operation. Variants of the guarded commands which were introduced in section 1.2.4.1 provide the mechanisms that enable operations to be delayed.

Within a procedure the sequence of operations is defined by four forms of guarded commands. DP uses the colon (:) instead of the left arrow ($\rightarrow$) to separate a guard from its guarded list, and a vertical bar (|) is used instead of the box ($\square$) to separate guarded statements. All forms of guarded command are terminated by the symbol **end**.

The usual conditional and repetitive forms of guarded commands are implemented by **if** and **do** statements. These simply evaluate the guards and select the guarded lists to be executed from the set with open guards. If there are no open guards in a repetitive command, control simply passes to the next statement. It is a program error for there not to be any open guards for a conditional command and the program will be aborted.

Two other forms of guarded command allow processes to wait for conditions to become true; they provide the mechanisms for process synchronisation. The 'when statement' has the form:-

when

      <guard> :

           <guarded_list>

|

      <guard> :

           <guarded_list>

      ...

end

The process waits until one of the guards becomes true and then it executes the corresponding guarded list. If no guards are open the process will wait until the actions of other processes change the values of variables so that a guard becomes open. The 'cycle statement' is the endless repetition of a 'when statement'; it has the form:-

cycle

      <guard> :

           <guarded_list>

|

      <guard> :

           <guarded_list>

      ...

end

An operation, either the *<initial_statement>* of a process or an external request, is executed until it terminates or becomes blocked at a **when** or **cycle** statement with no open guards. Control is then passed to another operation until it also terminates or becomes blocked. In this way the operations are executed under mutual exclusion, the hardware processor is multiplexed between the operations of a process under software control and not on a time-sliced basis. In this respect DP resembles Modula (section 3.4.3).

The operations within a process may interact only indirectly, by the modification of global variables which are used in the guards of other operations. There is no mechanism for direct coordination of operations within DP. This contrasts with CP, which uses queue operations for process synchronisation, and with CSP which uses synchronous message passing. A DP operation does not have a simple method of designating which of a set of possible operations will be the next to be executed; the underlying implementation makes a random selection from the set of pending remote procedure calls or delayed operations waiting with open guards. However, it is possible to impose a specific scheduling discipline within a process by explicitly programming its structure so that there is never more than one open guard at any one time.

Since the variables of a process may be accessed by several autonomous operations, the concept of a data invariant is also useful. Invariants were introduced for monitors in section 3.2.1; they require that the monitor's variables are always in a consistent state before a process relinquishes its exclusive access. In DP a context switch may occur at the end of each common procedure or at each **when** or **cycle** statement, so the invariant must be established at all of these points.

An operation that calls a remote operation does not release its current processor but waits for the remote operation to be completed and for any results to be returned; it then continues its operation. As calls to remote operations therefore waste processor resources, the minimum possible work should be done in this way. Assuming that the system is implemented on true multi-processor hardware, the maximum concurrency will be obtained if the local process performs as much of the work as is possible. Remote operations should be used to request the provision of a service or to retrieve a result. The program should thus be structured as a collection of processes providing services at the request of other client processes. This is the basic 'object-oriented' model where a single program component implements all the functions associated with a particular program abstraction.

Notice that, because an operation retains control of a process during the execution of a remote operation, it is possible for software to become deadlocked in just the same way as a system using nested monitor structures. The program design should ensure that there are no mutual dependencies between processes.

The lack of parametrised type definitions in DP is compensated in part by the provision of fixed length process arrays which provide several incarnations of the same process. The standard function *this* delivers the index of the calling process within the array and can be used to tailor the behaviour of individual processes.

5.2.1. Program examples

The logger example, that was introduced in section 2.2, cannot be implemented in DP simply as three processes communicating by remote operations because of the tight timing constraints of the input process. Processes change to another operation only when the active process becomes blocked. The guaranteed minimum response time to service a remote operation must be at least the maximum time between two **when** or **cycle** statements in any of the operations of that process. This problem is illustrated in the following example of an unsuitable structure for the *calculator* process. In the example, the remote operation *insert* is used to fill a buffer with data. When the buffer is full the data is analysed by the local process and the buffer is reset. The two operations are synchronised by the guards which test the value of the variable *buffer_full*.

```
process calculator;

var
        buffer_full        : boolean;
        buffer             : array[0..max_buf] of item;
        next_in            : 0..max_buf;

        proc insert; {called by inputter}
        when
                not buffer_full:
                        <deposit_data_in_buffer>;
                        buffer_full := next_in = max_buf;
                        if
                                not buffer_full :
                                        next_in := next_in + 1
                        end {if}
        end; {when}


begin   {calculator process}
        next_in := 0;
        buffer_full := false;
        cycle
                buffer_full:
                        <do_calculations>;
                        next_in := 0;
                        buffer_full := false;

                        <transmit_results>;
        end;
end;  {calculator}
```

The problem with this design is that the call to the *insert* operation may be delayed while the previous buffer of results is completely processed. This may be an acceptable mechanism between the *calculator* and the *storer* processes, but a small buffer process with a shorter response time is required between the *inputter* and the *calculator* processes. This buffer can be implemented by a process whose initial statement serves only to initialise the variables before it terminates. The process then continues to exist and to service the remote operations of the other processes. The overall program would therefore have the form:-

```
process inputter;
cycle
        input_available :              {guard set by hardware}
                <service_input_device>;
                call buffer.insert (data);
end;


process buffer;
var
        buff : array[0..max_buf] of item;
        next_in, next_out : 0..max_buf;
        count              : 0..max_buf + 1;

        proc insert (data : item);
        when
                count <= max_buf:          {room in buffer}
                        buff[next_in] := data;
                        next_in  := (next_in + 1) mod (max_buf + 1);
                        count    := count + 1    {insert and update}
        end;  {when and insert}

        proc extract (#data : item);
        when
                count > 0:                {data in buffer?}
                        data     := buff[next_out];
                        next_out := (next_out +1) mod (max_buf +1);
                        count    := count - 1;
        end;

begin   {initialise}
        next_in  := 0;
        next_out := 0;
        count    := 0;
end;    {of buffer process}


process calculator;
var
        lbuf : array[0..lmax_buf] of item;
        ...
```

```
do
        system_running:
                i := 0;
                do
                        i <= lmax_buf:   {room in local buffer}
                                call buffer.extract (#lbuf[i]);
                                i := i + 1        {update counter}
                end;
                <calculate_mean_and_std_dev>;
                call storer.insert (mean, std_dev)
end;  {calculator}


process storer;
var
        mean_buf, std_devbuf : array[0..omax_buf] of item;
        next_in              : 0..omax_buf;
        buffer_full          : boolean;

        proc insert (mean, std_dev : integer);
        when
                not buffer_full :                       {wait for room}
                        mean_buf[next_in]   := mean;  {insert results}
                        std_devbuf[next_in] := std_dev;
                        buffer_full := next_in = omax_buf;
                        if
                                not buffer_full:
                                        next_in := next_in + 1
                        end;  {if}
        end;  {non-cyclic buffer}

begin  {storer}
        buffer_full     := false;
        next_in         := 0;
        do
                system_running :                        {storer process}
                        when
                                buffer_full:      {wait for full buffer}
                                        <transmit_data>;
                                        buffer_full     := false;
                                        next_in         := 0
                        end
        end;  {system_running}
end;  {storer}
```

5.2.2. Carpark example

The carpark control is easily implemented in DP using two arrays of processes to control the input and output gates and a *space_control* process to coordinate the allocation of resources. The *exit_control* processes simply record the departure of a vehicle by calling a remote operation in *space_control*.

The *entrance_control* processes request the allocation of a space when a customer arrives; they include their identity (*this*) in the request in case no resources are immediately available. The boolean value returned indicates whether the request was satisfied, in which case the customer is admitted. If the request was queued, the customer is informed that there will be a delay and a second operation (*collect*) is called which blocks until a space is allocated and the customer can be admitted. The gate processes are outlined below.

```
process exit_control[n];
cycle
        waiting_car:
                <dismiss_leaver>;
                call space_control.depart;  {return the space}
end;


process entrance_control[n];
var
        ok : bool;
cycle
        waiting_car:
                call space_control.arrive (this # ok);
                if
                        ok:
                                <admit_customer>  {no problem}

                |
                        not ok:
                                <indicate_delay>; {delay expected}
                                call space_control.collect (this);
                                                {wait allocation}
                                <rescind_delay>;  {allocated now}
                                <admit_customer>
                end {if}
end;{cycle}
```

The *space_control* process contains a number of variables which are operated upon by the local process and by remote operations. The remote operations simply store requests for services and the local process provides the control and scheduling. The variable *returns* simply records the number of unprocessed spaces returned by *exit_control* processes. The variable *spaces* records the number of un-allocated spaces. If an *entrance_control* process calling the *arrive* operation finds that there are free spaces, it will allocate itself one and adjust the value of *spaces*. If no space is free, a request is posted in the array *requests* and the count of outstanding requests is incremented in the variable *waiting*.

The process later calls the operation *collect* which uses a **when** statement to wait for its request to be granted. The request may already have been granted by the time that *collect* operation is invoked, in which case the process will not be delayed. These remote operations are programmed as:-

```
process space_control;

const
        max_spaces = 100;

var
        returns, spaces   : 0..max_spaces;
        waiting           : 0..n;
        next              : 1..n;
        requests, grants  : array[n] bool;

        proc depart;                              {return space}
        returns := returns + 1;

        proc arrive (who : int # ok : bool);      {request space}
        if
                spaces > 0:                       {space available}
                        spaces  := spaces - 1;
                        ok      := true           {no problem}
        |
                spaces = 0:                       {full}
                        requests[who]  := true;  {lodge request}
                        ok             := false  {return disappointed}
        end;  {if}

        proc collect (who : int);                 {pick up a requested space}
        when
                grant[who]:                       {wait for allocation}
                        grant[who] := false       {reset request}
        end; {when}
```

The initialisation of the variables and the allocation of the resources is performed by the *space_control* process itself. Most of the time it is delayed at the beginning of a **cycle** statement waiting for resources to be returned; it then reallocates them. If there are no outstanding requests the resources are added to the general pool, otherwise the next outstanding request is satisfied.

The allocation strategy programmed here is not fifo. Instead, outstanding requests are serviced in a cyclical order. This policy is not strictly fair but does not result in process starvation. The initial statement of *space_control* is:-

```
begin
returns  := 0;
waiting  := 0;
spaces   := max_spaces;
next     := 1;
do
        next <= n:
                      requests[next]    := false;
                      grants[next]      := false;
                      next              := next + 1
end; {of initialisation}

cycle
returns > 0:
        if
                  waiting = 0:    {no waiting process}
                      spaces   := spaces + returns;
                                          {put returns up for grabs}
                      returns  := 0

        |
                  waiting > 0:    {waiting processes}
                         do       {find next request}
                         not requests[next]:
                                  if
                                       next = n:
                                               next := 1
                                  |
                                       next <> n:
                                               next := next + 1
                                  end
                         end;     {request found}
                         grants[next]       := true; {grant request}
                         requests[next]     := false;{remove request}
                         waiting            := waiting - 1;
                         returns            := returns - 1;
           end; {if}
    end; {cycle}
    end; {space_control}
```

5.3. SUMMARY OF DP

The examples demonstrate both the flexibility of program structures that are available with DP's remote operations, and the simplicity and elegance of the language. In contrast to CSP, process interaction in DP is asymmetric; the calling process knows the called process but not vice-versa. The ability of operations to return results combines well with this structure to provide 'client-server' program structures.

The static nature of the language means that a great deal of checking can be performed by the compiler and that the process interaction can be easily implemented. The compiler can determine which processes will invoke external requests to each process, and generate an anonymous 'representative process' for each external caller. These representatives simply intercept requests from their 'masters' and implement the operation on the local processor. The local representatives serve to store the values passed as parameters and to provide local working storage. They are manipulated by the underlying local scheduling algorithms.

A particular advantage of this scheme is that the scheduling provided by the guards in **cycle** and **when** statements can involve local parameter values as well as global variables, as is the case, for example, with the value of *who* in the *collect* operation of *space_control*. This is a significant enhancement over the process synchronisation provided by most monitor based languages.

Process interaction is much simpler to implement in DP than in CSP, because the interaction between processes is more indirect. DP processes coordinate their operation only indirectly, through shared variables, they do not interact directly with each-other's statement guards as they do in CSP. In DP a remote operation does not need the collaboration of the remote process in order to be executed and, furthermore, there is no way to rescind an operation once it is requested. The overall result is a much simpler implementation model.

The concept of 'remote procedure calls' introduced by DP has proved fruitful and it has been used in a number of distributed systems, as well as strongly influencing the design of Ada's rendezvous.

5.4. ADA AND THE RENDEZVOUS

Ada is the DoD's attempt to define a comprehensive real-time programming language suitable for use on the largest and most ambitious projects. Ada introduces very little that is new in language design; however, there is very little that it does not include. The result is rather awesome in its coverage and complexity, a level of complexity which has attracted severe criticism (e.g. Hoare 1981). This section will present only the minimum aspects of Ada necessary for the understanding of its process communication facility, the rendezvous. Complete introductions to programming in Ada can be found in the books by Stratford-Collins (1982) and Young (1984).

Processes in Ada are called tasks. They may be declared as single instances or in type definitions so that various instances can be dynamically created within a program. Ada goes further than most languages towards integrating tasks with other language objects. They can be declared as local variables within other tasks, either individually or as task arrays; created dynamically using access variables (which are Ada's pointer or reference variables); and can even be included as fields of records.

A task that has created other tasks is their 'parent' and they are 'dependent' tasks. The scope rules of Ada are very complex, but they do allow dependent tasks to access global data of their parent. However, the access is totally uncontrolled; mutual exclusion is *not* provided and tasks may retain working copies of variables in processor registers, so the use of global variables for task communication should be avoided.

Safe process coordination is provided by the rendezvous, which is a synchronised remote procedure call. A rendezvous is an asymmetric relationship between a pair of processes where the 'client' process requests a specific 'server' process to perform some operation on its behalf. The client is delayed until the server chooses to perform the operation, at which point the rendezvous is said to occur. On completion of the operation the processes proceed independently. If there are no outstanding requests the server can be delayed and wait for one. The relationship between the tasks is asymmetric in that the client process must explicitly specify which task is to provide the service whilst the server does not specify the identity of the client and it will accept a suitable request from any task; in fact, the server is unaware of the identity of the client.

The rendezvous provides process synchronisation. Mutual exclusion can be provided by encapsulating data structures within a server process and ensuring that all accesses of the data are implemented by the server in response to requests. This enforces a serial ordering of requests and eliminates any problems of interference through uncontrolled access.

The operations provided by a task are defined as named entries, which may be parametrised in the same way as procedures. Ada was designed for the development of large systems, so it has facilities which allow modules to be compiled separately and linked together later. This requires modules, such as tasks, to be defined in two parts: the 'specification', which defines the component's interface which is accessible to other program components; and the 'body', which contains the private components consisting of local variables and program code. The specification of a task defines which services are offered, in terms of a series of entries; the body defines how these services are implemented. A task specification takes the form:-

```
task <task_name> is
        entry <entry_name_1> (<parameters>);
        entry <entry_name_2> (<parameters>);
        ...
end <task_name>;
```

Entry parameters take the same form as procedure parameters and specify the parameters' names and their types. There are three modes of parameters:

in: The parameter acts as a local constant whose value is given by the actual parameter supplied with the call.

out: The parameter acts as a local variable whose value is assigned to the actual parameter when the procedure or rendezvous terminates.

in out:
The parameter acts like an initialised local variable and also allows the updating of the actual parameter that is supplied.

The **in** mode is assumed by default. The specification of a typical buffer task would take the form:-

```
task buffer is
        entry insert      (i : in  item);
        entry extract     (i : out item);
end buffer;
```

This declares a specific task named *buffer* whose entries can be accessed by other tasks using the familiar notation for a remote operation, i.e.

```
buffer.insert (data);
```

If the keyword **type** is included after **task** in the specification, the result is a type definition which may later be instantiated as a number of similar task variables, e.g.

```
task type buffer is
        ...
end buffer;
        ...
buf_1, buf_2 : buffer;
```

The implementation of the task is specified in the body definition which has the form:-

```
task body <task_name> is

<declarations>

begin
        <sequence_of_statements>;
end <task_name>;
```

The *<declarations>* section contains the definitions of types, variables or procedures local to the task, and also the declarations of any dependent tasks. The operation of the task is specified by the *<sequence_of_statements>* which is executed once the declarations have been elaborated. Ada includes all the usual repetitive and conditional statements in the form of for, while, if and case statements, together with assignment statements, procedure calls and compound statements.

Within the task body the rendezvouses are implemented by 'accept statements' which specify when an entry call will be serviced. An accept statement has the form:-

> **accept** *<entry_name> (<parameters>)*
> **do**
>   *<sequence_of_statements>*
> **end** *<entry_name>;*

where the *<entry_name>* and its parameters must correspond with an entry declared in the specification part of the task. When control reaches the accept statement it will execute the *<sequence_of_statements>* on behalf of a task which has made a call to the corresponding entry using the parameters supplied by the client. At the end of the rendezvous any values of **out** parameters are copied back to the client and the local copies of the parameters cease to exist. The two tasks then proceed independently.

The rendezvous may be used simply for synchronisation, in which case the

> **do**
>   *<sequence_of_statements>*
> **end** *<entry_name>;*

clause can be completely omitted. The two tasks proceed independently immediately the accept statement is completed. If there are no outstanding calls for an accept statement the server will wait for one. If a number of tasks call the same entry faster than they are accepted by the server the requests will be queued and the client tasks will be delayed. Each accept statement will service the request at the front of its associated entry queue. The server task may contain several accept statements for the same entry, and these may implement the function in different ways. The client task has no influence over the point at which its request is serviced or the manner in which the service is implemented.

Previous examples have demonstrated the need for flexibility within patterns of communication; to provide this flexibility, the synchronous nature of the accept statement is supplemented by the 'select statement', which is Ada's variant of 'guarded commands' (see section 1.2.4.1). Select statements are associated only with a rendezvous and cannot be used elsewhere in a program. However, the inclusion of some additional features together with restrictions on their combined usage has turned Dijkstra's elegant constructs into baroque edifices.

The basic form of the select statement for a server task is:-

```
select
        when <boolean_expression> =>
                accept <entry_name> (<parameters>);
                        ...
                end <entry_name>;
                <sequence_of_statements>

or
        when <boolean_expression> =>
                accept <entry_name> (<parameters>);
                        ...
                end <entry_name>
                <sequence_of_statements>
        ...

else
        <sequence_of_statements>;
end select;
```

The guards are simple boolean expressions defined in terms of the task's environment; the guard may be omitted for an entry that is always open. The execution of a select statement proceeds in the following manner. Each guard is evaluated to determine the set of open guards. From the set of open accept statements, one with a pending entry call is selected for execution. After the rendezvous has been completed and any associated statements have been executed, the select statement terminates.

If there are no open entries with pending calls, the 'else' clause is executed, if one has been provided. Otherwise, a 'program-error' occurs and either the task will terminate or some user-defined error recovery procedures will be invoked.

If there are open guards but no pending calls, then the else clause is executed if it exists; if there is no 'else clause' the task simply waits until an eligible call occurs. However, the guards are not re-evaluated, so if the environment is changed it will not affect the set of entry calls which will be accepted. The use of the select statement is demonstrated in Fig. 5.1, which gives a program example of the familiar cyclic buffer. Ada comments are prefixed by two minus signs (--). The guards protect the buffer from overflow or underflow by ensuring that suitable conditions hold before accepting a rendezvous. The minimum work is done during the rendezvous and the local variables are updated afterwards; this is aimed at maximising the potential parallelism of the system.

Two other constructs can be used instead of accept options in a select statement within a server task. The 'delay' option allows the programming of suitable actions if no entries are called within a given time - a useful facility in real-time systems - and the 'terminate' option allows the programming of the orderly termination of groups of related tasks. These options will not be

```
task body buffer is

max_buf : constant integer := 63;
bufsize  : constant integer := 64;
buf      : array (0..max_buf) of item;
count    : integer range 0..bufsize := 0;
next_in, next_out : integer range 0..max_buf := 0;

begin
loop
        select
                when count < bufsize =>          --room in buffer
                        accept insert (i : in item);
                                buf(next_in) := i;
                        end insert;               --end rendezvous
                        next_in := (next_in + 1) mod bufsize;
                        count  := count + 1;

        or                                        --next select option
                when count > 0 =>                 --data in buffer
                        accept extract (i : out item);
                                i := buf(next_out);
                        end extract;
                        next_out := (next_out + 1) mod bufsize;
                        count   := count - 1;

        end select;
end loop;
end buffer;
```

Fig. 5.1 - Cyclic buffer in Ada.

discussed further here.

A select statement can also be used by a client task to avoid becoming delayed waiting for a rendezvous. The 'conditional entry call' takes the form:-

> **select**
> > *<entry_call>;*
> > *<sequence_of_statements>;*
> **else**
> > *<sequence_of_statements>;*
> **end select;**

The entry call is made only if the server is ready to accept the call immediately, otherwise the 'else' clause is executed. Alternatively the 'timed entry call' can be used; this allows a rendezvous to be aborted if it is not accepted within a specified period. It has the form:-

> **select**
> > *<entry_call>;*
> > *<sequence_of_statements>;*
> **or**
> > **delay** *<period>;*
> > *<sequence_of_statements>;*
> **end select;**

The select statement takes different forms depending on whether it is used in server or in client tasks. A server can wait to accept a rendezvous on a set of open entries. However, a client task can wait only at one entry at a time; the select statement gives the option only of aborting a rendezvous. This is analogous to the restriction in CSP, which allows input commands to be used in guards but prohibits the use of output commands in guards. There is no way to combine accept statements and entry calls in one select statement: a task cannot be a client and a server simultaneously.

5.4.1. Program examples

The tight synchronisation of the rendezvous means that buffers must be inserted between the three tasks of the data-logger example. These buffers must take the form of extra tasks similar to the one outlined previously in Fig. 5.1.·

Implementing the carpark controller in Ada is trivially simple because the language contains built-in features ideally suited to solving this form of problem. Three different task types are required; entrance and exit controllers and the central coordinator. Ada uses the rendezvous mechanism to synchronise tasks with hardware signals so it can be used to detect the presence of cars waiting to enter or leave. This interface between the hardware and the software is dealt with in more detail in chapter 7.

The *exit_control* tasks take the form:-

```
task type exit_control is
        entry car_leaving;  -- hardware interface
end task;

task body exit_control is
begin
        loop
                accept car_leaving;                 -- wait for car
                        <reset_hardware>;
                end car_leaving;
                space_control.depart;               -- return space
                <dismiss_car>;
        end loop;
end exit_control;
```

The *space_control* task is very simple, it keeps track of the number of allocated spaces and only accepts a rendezvous with an *entrance_control* task if there are free spaces;

```
task space_control is
        entry arrive;
        entry depart;
end space_control;

task body space_control is
max_spaces      : constant integer := 200;
spaces          : integer range 0..max_spaces := max_spaces;
begin
        loop
                select
                        accept depart;              --entry always open
                        spaces := spaces + 1;       --update count
                or
                        when spaces > 0 =>          --only if room
                                accept arrive;
                                spaces := spaces - 1;
                end select;
        end loop;
end space_control;
```

The *entrance_control* task uses a rendezvous to synchronise its operation with the hardware and to detect when a car arrives. It then attempts to rendezvous with the *space_control*; however, if the carpark is full this will fail and the else clause is executed. The *entrance_control* task then informs the customer that the carpark is full and makes an unconditional call to the *space_control*. This call will be delayed in the entrance queue until spaces are returned and the rendezvous is accepted. The definition of the *entrance_control* tasks is:-

> **task type** *entrance_control* **is**
> > **entry** *car_arriving;*
>
> **end** *entrance;*

> **task body** *entrance_control* **is**
> **begin**
> > **loop**
> > > **accept** *car_arriving;*
> > > > *<reset_hardware>;*
> > >
> > > **end** *car_arriving;*
> > >
> > > **select**   *--conditional entry call*
> > > > *space_control.arrive;*
> > >
> > > **else**
> > > > *<indicate_delay>;*   *--if entry not ready*
> > > > *space_control.arrive;*   *--wait this time*
> > > > *<rescind_delay>;*
> > >
> > > **end select***;*
> > >
> > > *<admit_car>;*
> >
> > **end loop***;*
>
> **end** *entrance_control;*

The solution is extremely simple because the language indirectly passes information about the state of the *space_control* back to the *entrance_control* task in the conditional entry call. This enables the *entrance_control* task to inform the customer that there will be a delay before the task is committed to a rendezvous. The solution is also simplified because the entry queues are defined as being fifo and queuing in them is an acceptable program technique; this automatically provides the scheduling for the reallocation of spaces as they are returned.

If a different discipline is required it can be implemented a using a 'family' or array of entries in *space_control*. Client and server tasks select one of the entries for a rendezvous using a constant or variable. Assuming that the *entrance_control* tasks are declared in an array and that the *space_control* task has an array of *arrive* entries, then each *entrance_control* could select a unique entry queue to *space_control. space_control* could then implement any scheduling strategy required. For example, it could attempt to service each gate in turn using the following program:-

```
task space_control is
        entry arrive (1..max_gates);
        entry depart;
end space_control;

task body space_control is
        ...
begin
        loop
                for i in 1..max_gates loop
                        select
                                accept depart;    --always open
                                spaces := spaces + 1;
                        or
                                when spaces > 0 =>       --if room
                                        accept arrive(i); --try this
                                                spaces := spaces -1;
                        else
                                null;              --else do nothing
                        end select;
                end loop;                  --and try next gate
                delay 1;                   --have a break
        end loop                           --start again
end space_control;
```

The task loops around each element of the entry array attempting a rendezvous, and if there are no outstanding requests from a particular gate the else
option is taken to allow next entry to be tried. After polling each entry, the
task delays for 1 second to prevent it wasting too much processor time.
Notice that accepting a *depart* entry will deprive the current *arrive* entry of
its opportunity to rendezvous.

5.4.2. Summary and discussion of Ada

The previous sections have provided a brief introduction to process coordination in Ada. The comprehensive and extensive facilities and the inclusion of
time-outs go beyond most other proposals. However, the tasking facilities are
not very well integrated into the rest of the language and give the impression
of having been grafted on as an afterthought; in fact the conditional and
timed entry calls are late additions.

The rendezvous is a useful coordination concept, allowing the
specification of quite sophisticated ordering constraints for process interaction
and a comprehensive and flexible parameter passing mechanism in both directions. However, its synchronous nature has been criticised because it tends to
lead to system designs requiring more processes than are needed in asynchronous monitor-based systems. The presence of the additional buffer processes
imply greater overheads in terms of processor context swaps. However,

there is little current evidence concerning the extent of these overheads or how various techniques compare.

The asymmetric nature of the rendezvous has also been criticised; it is usually argued that it is an advantage because a server task does not need to know who it is serving. However, this may represent a security weakness in the language since a server is unable to identify its client and so cannot check the validity or legitimacy of requests; for example, a resource allocation process can not verify that a request to release a particular resource originates from the current owner.

The language is open to subtle timing faults because of its shared data and the time taken to implement select statements and to implement a rendezvous. The most obvious source of potential errors is the provision of unprotected shared data. This feature is retained because some designers argue that it is needed in some applications to achieve real-time access to large amounts of data, for instance in radar systems. It is assumed that anyone willing to resort to the facilities will also be aware of the potential problems. However, the rendezvous mechanisms can interact with these facilities to provide additional scope for the usual interference problems. For example, a remote call evaluates its arguments when the call is made, not when it is accepted. This means that there may be a considerable delay between the formulation of a request and its implementation, providing ample opportunity for another task to invalidate the parameters. Problems may also be introduced on the server's side, since a task evaluates the guards to a select statement only once. If there are no pending calls to open guards the task may be delayed for some time and this may allow another task to invalidate the conditions implied by some guards.

Similar subtle problems may arise from the use of the 'attributes' feature. The attributes are pre-defined mechanisms which allow a task to examine the program environment during execution; for example, they may be used to determine the actual bounds of a variable sized array. The value of an attribute a about an entity e in a program is delivered by writing $e'a$. For example, a boolean attribute *callable* is defined for tasks; its returned value indicates whether a task has been activated and not yet terminated. A cautious programmer might include the test:-

```
if space_control'callable then
        space_control.depart
else
        temp := temp + 1
end if;
```

This attempts to avoid the generation of the program error which would result from a call to a non-existent task by checking that a task exists before calling it. However, there is no guarantee that *space_control* will not terminate before engaging in the rendezvous.

Attributes may cause similar errors on the server side of a rendezvous. The *count* attribute delivers as its result the number of tasks waiting at an entry. A task might hope to avoid becoming delayed by using the following statements to ensure that there is an outstanding call before being committed to a rendezvous.

> **select**
>
> > **when** *depart' count > 0* **and** *space = 0* =>
> >   **accept** *depart;*
>
> **or**
>
> > ...
>
> **end select***;*

Unfortunately this is not entirely safe, since a client task may use the timed entry construct, and decide to withdraw its request in the period between the server evaluating its guard and accepting the rendezvous.

The final judgement of Ada is yet to come; the slow development of its compilers and the complexity of the language have limited its impact so far. Whatever the conclusion, its impact is likely to be substantial; the previous language sponsored by DoD was Cobol!

5.5. SUMMARY OF OPERATION ORIENTATED SYSTEMS

DP introduced the concept of remote procedure calls which implement operations on encapsulated data structures. In DP the local process is redundant in some cases but can be used to maximise parallelism in a true multiprocessor system. Remote calls in DP are immediately eligible for execution, any synchronisation constraints being expressed within each procedure by guarded commands. Guards may refer to parameters of the call and to the global variables of the object, but not to the parameters of other calls.

DP programs are essentially 'distributed' programs; they lack centralised control or co-ordination and rely on the mutual co-operation of the component processes. Unfortunately, this distribution sometimes makes the operation of modules more difficult to understand since it may depend on the interaction between a number of concurrent procedure activations. Although the remote operations are synchronised with the calling process, the overall system is asynchronous since processes interact only indirectly, through shared variables.

Ada imposes more discipline upon programs by casting processes into a client/server relationship. The ordering of operations on encapsulated data is strictly controlled and is conveniently expressed in the body of the server task. Ada programs, therefore, can be more readily comprehensible, although less aesthetically pleasing; bad design or bad programming may render them unintelligible of course. A weakness of Ada, in comparison with DP, is that the parameters to entry calls are not accessible to the server task when it is selecting a rendezvous. Once a rendezvous has been accepted the server is obliged to complete it even if the parameters to the call reveal that it was an

unfortunate choice. The facility of having 'families of entries' provides a
partial solution by allowing the server more discrimination in the acceptance
of entries. Unfortunately, when a wide range of entries may be accepted, the
restricted methods of specifying which entries to accept leads either to a very
cumbersome program structure or to an inefficient polling implementation.
Allowing sets of entries to be accepted would greatly enhance their utility,
i.e.

    accept REQUEST (7..10)

Ada was developed with the intention of it becoming a standard
language, not as a research tool. Any future changes are expected to be
minor revisions or clarifications and not radical changes. However, some
workers are still exploring ways of enhancing the rendezvous concept.

The language SR (Synchronised Resources) (Andrews, 1981,1982)
evolved at the same time as Ada, and was subjected to the same influences.
It introduced some new ideas in data and program structures as well as two
new ideas in process coordination. SR retains the concept of parametrised
entries which are accepted by a server process, but it allows them to be
invoked in two ways.

(1)   A process may **call** an entry in another process, in which case the entry
       is implemented as a rendezvous and the two processes are synchronised
       during the execution of the remote operation.

(2)   A process may **send** an operation to an entry, in which case the client
       is not delayed. This option is restricted to entries which only have **in**
       parameters, so no results can be returned. This option avoids imposing
       unnecessary synchronisation on a program; for instance, the message
       that a vehicle is leaving the carpark is an ideal candidate for a **send**
       operation. This form of interaction is analogous to an asynchronous
       message system.

SR also enhances the server side of the rendezvous to provide greater
flexibility in choosing which call to accept. A group of entries may be
selected using a guarded command of the form:-

    in

        <entry_name> (<parameters>)
            and   <boolean_expression>
            by   <integer_expression>
              ->

                       <sequence_of_statements>
    □
            ...
    ni

The <boolean_expression> acts as a guard for any requests queued in the
entry; its specification is located after the entry in order that it may have
access to the parameters of the requests as well as to the global variables.

This allows guards to be more selective about the requests that are accepted. SR entry queues are not fifo, and any pending request may become eligible for acceptance. The relative priority of the eligible requests may be established using the *integer_expression*, which provides the scheduling once the logical validity of options has been established. Both the 'and clauses' and the 'by clauses' are optional and can be omitted to give an Ada-like rendezvous.

A different set of extensions are proposed in Cell (Silberschatz, 1984).

(1)   An optional 'from <task>' clause is added to the accept statement to make the client/server relationship more symmetrical.

(2)   The execution of a rendezvous can be suspended using an 'await statement'. This statement evaluates a boolean expression which can contain parameters to the rendezvous. If the evaluation of the expression yields the value false the context of the rendezvous is saved and the server exits from the accept statement. The rendezvous may be resumed later if the server returns to the enclosing select statement, at which point await statements with delayed clients are treated like guards. This ability to delay and resume external requests gives many of the facilities of DP's asynchronous procedure calls.

(3)   Cell allows the partial ordering of options to a select statement by specifying the relative priority of pairs of options. The accept and await statements can be labelled (e.g. L1:, L2:, L3: etc.), and their relative priorities can then be specified in an 'order' statement, e.g.

order (L1>L2, L1>L3);

This allows the programmer to specify priorities when required (e.g. L1 highest priority), but it allows the system to make an arbitrary choice where no priority is specified (e.g. between L2 and L3).

The extra facilities of both SR and Cell have been shown to simplify the programming of some commonly used scheduling policies. The price of this advantage is paid in the added complexity of the language definition, the compiler and the run-time support. In this respect the proposals mirror both authors' earlier work on extensions to CP (Andrews, 1977; Silberschatz, 1977). The proposals may serve best as catalysts which will affect the next generation of languages, rather than being regarded as language proposals *per se*.

6

Comparison of Methods

6.1. INTRODUCTION

Each of the three previous chapters have introduced one of the major paradigms for implementing concurrent programs: protected shared data in the form of monitors, message based interactions and remote operations. Message-based systems and those using remote-operations can both be subdivided into synchronous and asynchronous systems; monitor based systems are essentially asynchronous. This gives five major styles of programs which have been examined using the languages CP, PLITS, CSP, DP and Ada. This chapter will compare the use of these languages and will demonstrate the relationships between the relevant features found in each.

The designers of these languages had dissimilar goals and produced languages with dissimilar characteristics. CP and DP are both intended as systems implementation languages, so their inherent design aims are to minimise the need for underlying support software and to provide a more convenient medium than assembler code in which to program higher level features. In contrast, other languages contain higher level features which require extensive underlying support; these features might well be implemented using one of these two systems implementation languages. For example, the message buffering of PLITS might well be implemented using a language like CP. Although high-level features are often convenient for the application programmer, they may involve an excessive overhead when they provide more facilities than are needed by a particular application. High level features also impose greater constraints on the programmer by establishing the implementation policy.

The programming examples of the data-logger and carpark controller have served to demonstrate the need for several facilities in a concurrent language:-

Coordination,
>   processes need to be able to agree on some aspects of the program's status; for example, the values of some variables.

Communication,
>   for information exchange between processes.

Synchronisation,
>   to enforce logical constraints on the progress of processes.

Nondeterminism,
>   processes, or groups of processes, need to be able to express nondeterminate operation since their progress may be controlled by unknown or unpredictable external influences.

Table 6.1 summarises the features of each language which satisfy these requirements. Each language will now be considered in more detail.

6.2. CP

Of the languages discussed in this text, only CP has two distinct types of permanent system elements, **processes** and **monitors**. Monitors can be used to provide both co-ordination and communication. The protected variables of a monitor provide safe, coordinated access to common program variables. CP does not support inter-process communication directly, but various patterns of communication can be established by implementing protocols within a program.

Comparison of language features				
	communication	synchronization	nondeterminism	determinism
CP	shared variables in monitors	queues	random access	programmed
PLITS	message	transaction or id	general receive	pending
CSP	synchronous message	inherent	guarded receive	programmed in guards
DP	shared variables and RPC	guards in process	inherent	programmed in guards
ADA	rendezvous	rendezvous	select	guards

Table 6.1 - Comparison of language features.

CP inherently is an asynchronous language. All processes compete for access to monitors, and access is granted on a fifo basis. The time taken to access a monitor is intended to be short in comparison with the timescale of events external to the system. For this reason a process is committed to completing a monitor call once it has initiated one; there are no facilities for it to abandon an entry request or to wait for one of several monitors to become available.

Where synchronisation is needed, a *queue* variable can be used. This provides a very primitive method of synchronisation between asynchronous processes; neither partner in the exchange knows the identity of the other.

Implementing the data-logger in CP requires the explicit programming of inter-process buffers to provide the communication routes between the three processes. These are quite easy and efficient to implement, provided that fixed length buffers are adequate.

The examples given in Chapter 3 did not give a detailed solution to the carpark control system to the extent of providing information to the customers concerning possible delays. However, the reader should be adequately familiar with the problem to appreciate that the solution will require the *entrance_control* to employ a protocol of monitor calls to lodge its request and then await its fulfilment in a user-defined queuing structure. Each time a customer departs, the *exit_control* must determine whether there is a waiting *entrance_control* which needs to be informed that it can proceed. Care must be taken that interleaving *entrance_control* and *exit_control* operations does not result in the loss of a parking space.

The solution program is more complex in CP than in the other languages since the tools provided are more primitive. Expanding the semantics of the *queue* variable to be a fifo multi-queue, like CE's and Mesa's *conditions* and Modula's *signals*, saves considerable complexity in this and in many similar cases, at very little additional cost to the implementation.

6.3. PLITS

PLITS programs have one form of permanent construct, the module, which is a process. During their execution these are supplemented by numerous, dynamically created and short-lived messages. Since there are no shared variables, coordination is provided by caretaker modules which control and disseminate the values of variables of interest to groups of modules. Thus coordination and communication take the form of message exchange for which extensive support is provided by the underlying software.

PLITS communication is asynchronous and messages are buffered until their destination module is willing to accept them. The general **receive** operation provides non-determinism by accepting any message directed to the module. The non-determinism can be reduced by specifying a particular partner to a communication and can be further reduced by specifying a **transaction** code which can be used to identify a unique message. These features can be combined to implement protocols that lead to synchronous or deterministic programs where necessary.

A module is unable to cancel or abort a **receive** operation once it has been initiated. However, if it is crucial that a module is not delayed waiting for a particular message it can examine the available messages using the **pending** function. The wide range of facilities available to the programmer can be combined to implement a spectrum of designs ranging from 'event driven' to 'polled' systems.

Despite the wide variety of operations on messages, the underlying implementation model is simple. The destination of each message is uniquely defined, so the message can be attached to the queue of pending messages associated with its destination module. Once the message has been sent, the originator is incapable of rescinding the message or affecting it in any way. The implementation is merely required to queue messages and to be able to inspect their contents in order to implement the selective receipt of messages which come from a specific source or which contain a specific transaction key.

The implementation of the data-logger in PLITS, which is given in Fig. 4.1, is trivially simple as a result of the close match between the problem requirements and the language constructs. The difficult part, that of providing asynchronous, buffered communication between processes, is performed by the underlying implementation.

The implementation of the carpark, given in Fig. 4.4, is also simple in PLITS because of two factors. Firstly, when compared with the CP solution, the degree of non-determinism within the program is reduced. The increase in determinism arises because the *space_control* module is an active agent which can deal with each transaction to its conclusion before allowing the next to proceed. This serialises the operations of *entrance_control* and *exit_control* modules and eliminates the interleaving of their actions. Other potential sources of error are avoided by synchronising the operation of *entrance_control* by including **from** clauses in its **receive** operations. The second factor leading to a simple design is the use of the underlying fifo message queuing mechanism of the *queuer* module to maintain the queue of outstanding requests for entry.

6.4. CSP

CSP is also based on message exchange between processes, but the synchronous nature of the communication means that the messages lack the autonomous existence within the buffering implementation of PLITS messages. Coordination is again provided by caretaker processes and all communication is implemented directly by the message exchange mechanism.

Message exchange is strictly synchronous and involves the co-operation of both parties to the exchange. Non-determinism is introduced in the form of guarded commands which can include a message-receipt operation in a guard; this mechanism allows a process to wait for communication from one of a number of processes.

The synchronous nature of communication and the use of input guards incur some overhead, since the receiving process must first establish which processes are available for communication; the actual partner is then selected from the set of possible partners and an acknowledgement must be sent to the chosen process to confirm the message exchange.

If guards are prohibited in output commands, a process is committed to completing a message exchange once it initiates an output statement. There is no mechanism by which it can rescind the commitment, and a simple implementation is possible. The suggested extension of allowing output commands to appear in guards, so that neither party will become committed to a communication, increases the complexity of the implementation to a virtually impractical degree. Without output guards CSP is quite easy and efficient to implement on a uniprocessor system, since there are none of the problems of message queuing or buffer management involved.

CSP's synchronous communication does not fit with the asynchronous nature of the data-logger and requires buffer processes for its implementation, which is shown in Fig. 4.5. The lack of output guards means that a process must send a request message and wait for a response in order to extract a message from the buffer. Thus the simple exchange of information from *inputter* to *calculator* involves three **send** and three **receive** operations. Thus the penalty of a simple implementation model is a more complex application program.

The carpark control is quite simple to implement. The example program given in Fig. 4.6 is intended to demonstrate the use of arrays of guards, but it could easily be expanded to have a similar structure to the PLITS version. The nature of this problem involves dialogues between the *entrance_control* and *space_control*. These do not need to be synchronised exactly so the provision of the synchronism is an unnecessary overhead in this case.

6.5. DP

Coordination in DP is provided by the remote procedure call mechanism which allows one process to access another's variables under conditions of mutual exclusion. DP does not provide any direct means of communication; this must be implemented indirectly using commonly accessible variables. Similarly, there is no direct synchronisation between processes. A process is directly synchronised with any remote operations that it invokes in another process, but these operations are coordinated only loosely with their defining process or with any other remote operations active in the same process. Operations within a process definition are essentially asynchronous, with the constraint that only one will be active at a time. This simplifies programming by enforcing mutual exclusion of access to the variables of a process.

Guarded commands are used to determine when a process is eligible for execution, and the ordering of execution is non-deterministic. Where synchronisation or determinism are specifically required they can be imposed by the programmer through the careful programming of the guards to restrict the number of eligible processes.

The non-deterministic operation, and the fact that a process does not relinquish its exclusive access to local variables on remote calls means that some program structures can lead to long or indeterminate response times. These characteristics necessitate the inclusion of a buffer process between the *inputter* and the *calculator* in the logger example to ensure the fast, predictable response of the *inputter*. Where the constraints are less demanding, such as between the *calculator* and the *storer*, direct communication by remote operations is possible.

The structure of the carpark controller is quite satisfactory and most of the control functions are integrated into the one *space_control* module. However, the inherent non-determinism of the language does make it quite difficult to design or understand programs.

6.6. ADA

In Ada, **tasks** provide coordinated access to data, by encapsulating varibles, and by implementing operations on them at the request of other tasks. The rendezvous mechanism provides bidirectional communication between a pair of tasks, in which the client passes information to the server task and can subsequently receive information back. To the client, the rendezvous is an indivisible operation; to the server, it is structured and can involve substantial computational effort from initiation to completion.

The relationship between the client and server tasks is very asymmetric. The client must identify the server explicitly, but the server does not know the identity of the client. The same relationship is also found in CP and DP. Another aspect of this asymmetry is that the client does not know how the server will implement the operation. A server task definition can contain several **accept** statements which implement the same entry using different algorithms. The client has no influence over which of the services will be provided.

The rendezvous also provides process synchronisation; both parties must be ready for it to proceed and either can be delayed waiting for the other. The completion of the rendezvous is also synchronised.

Non-determinism is introduced in Ada using guarded commands in the form of **select** statements. These can be used by either, or both, parties to a rendezvous. A server uses the non-determinism to make several services available simultaneously and to accept whichever rendezvous is requested. A client can use **select** statements to avoid being committed to a rendezvous indefinitely and can withdraw from the rendezvous if the server is not ready immediately or if it does not accept the call within some specified period.

However, a client cannot use a **select** statement to solicit several rendez-vouses simultaneously and has to poll the server tasks continuously until one responds.

The synchronous nature of the rendezvous means that the logger example needs to include buffer tasks between the three major functions. These buffers, shown in Fig. 5.1, are easy to implement using the **select** statement.

The implementation of the carpark example is easier in Ada than in any of the other languages. This is because the high semantic content of the **select** statements and of the rendezvous happens to be well matched to the requirements of the problem. The *space_control* can indicate when the car-park is full by closing the guard on an entry, and the *entrance_control* task can detect this situation using a conditional entry call. Thus the underlying implementation automatically provides the initial dialogue between an *entrance_control* and *space_control* to establish whether there is any room available. This dialogue needed to be explicitly programmed in the other languages. The other useful concordance in semantics lies in the fact that tasks can have several entries dedicated to different functions and each entry has its own fifo queue. Thus entry queues can be used in scheduling, whereas monitors have only a single entry queue and the programmer is required to implement the queuing of requests.

Although Ada copes well with these two examples it does have problems. The most serious are that a server cannot access the parameters to a rendezvous before it has accepted it, and that once the rendezvous has begun it cannot be suspended or aborted. This means that a task may need to provide a large number of entries in order to constrain the range of parameters that each entry expects to service.

6.7. SUMMARY

The paradigms of process coordination lead to different ways of organising programs. These organisational structures can be illustrated by an analogy describing the ways of getting a photographic film developed and printed.

In a monitor styled system the photographer (a process) takes the film to a dark room (a monitor) to which he has access and develops the film for himself. There must be a lock on the dark-room door to prevent other photo-graphers entering to develop their own films and disturbing the occupant. Before leaving, each photographer must tidy up and put the light-sensitive chemicals away before allowing another photographer to enter (i.e. must re-establish the monitor invariant). The system provides the tools or resources and the processes do their own work.

An asynchronous message system leads to an organisation like a postal film laboratory, in which a process or group of processes offers a specialist service. The photographer process sends the film, together with the return address, to a known film developer. The photographer then proceeds with other jobs while the film is developed and sent back in the mail. At some later stage the photographer finds that the film has been returned and can continue working with it. If he has nothing else to do, the photographer can simply go to sleep until the film is returned and he is awakened by the postman.

The synchronous message system corresponds to the local one-man photographic shop. The photographer takes the film to the shop and waits for service by the proprietor who accepts the film. The photographer can then proceed with other work until he needs the prints at which point he must wait at home for the proprietor. Meanwhile, the proprietor develops the film and then makes a special delivery to the photographer's home. Eventually the two processes will meet and the films will be returned.

The asynchronous operation-oriented system corresponds to a more informal service. Photographers call in at the shop and leave work on the counter. The proprietor picks up the film, processes it and leaves the finished goods to be collected by the photographer.

Finally, the rendezvous scheme is analogous to a 'while you wait' service, where the photographer waits at the shop while the film is accepted, processed and then immediately returned.

Whichever organisational structure is chosen, the bulk of the work that needs to be performed remains the same. The differences lie in the way in which the work is distributed between the underlying language implementation and the processes within the application program. Table 6.2 summarises the suitability of each of the example languages for implementing the two example programs.

A more extensive set of comparisons have been performed between CSP, DP and Ada (Welsh, 1981). A suit of 16 applications were programmed in each language and the results compared. None of the languages established an overall advantage and, predictably, different language features

Comparison of examples		
	Data-logger	Car-park
CP	need to program buffers	problems with nested structure
PLITS	simple	good structure with 4 modules
CSP	need to program buffers	good structure
DP	need 1 buffer due to nondeterminism	good but complex to understand
ADA	need buffer tasks	simple

Table 6.2 - Comparison of suitability of languages for examples

proved more suitable for particular problems. A more definite observation was that:-

> "The example programs chosen by Hoare and Brinch Hansen do not strongly support the use of non-determinism for anything other than process communication, and it seems that the deterministic constructs of Ada would express the programmers' intent more succinctly in most cases. If the non-deterministic constructs are to be defended it must be on the grounds of uniform programming methodology rather than the frequency with which they provide greater expressive power."

The results of comparative studies suggest that it is pointless to seek universal solutions in a single language. A better approach may be to develop families of tools tailored to classes of problems. Language developers should be looking towards extensible systems in which it is easy to tailor a suitable working environment and to exploit previous work by re-using tools and techniques already available. These features are as much a function of the 'program support environment' as the language used for programming.

Part III

The Pragmatics

The final part of this book moves away from abstract models of processes and tackles some pragmatic issues concerning their implementation. Chapter 7 examines the relationship between software processes and the underlying hardware. It also considers the way the processor interfaces to the external environment through its peripheral devices.

Finally, Chapter 8 examines some of the implications of moving from a single processor system to the programming of a distributed system of communicating processors.

7

Interfacing to
Peripheral Devices

7.1. INTRODUCTION

This chapter will examine the way in which the hardware peripheral devices of a computer system are controlled by the software; it will illustrate the way in which the concepts of cooperating processes can be applied across the hardware-software boundary. Being concerned with this lower-level interface, the chapter needs to introduce some more details of the hardware and machine-level architecture. However, the aim of the chapter is to focus on higher-level concepts that permit the general organisation of systems to be managed properly. The chapter will, therefore, concentrate on those hardware aspects that are relevant to this aim.

Computer manufacturers usually emphasise the differences in the internal architecture of computers. However, in practice these differences are less significant than the similarities between machines. This chapter will, therefore, consider the structure of a 'typical' processor without digressing too much into the peculiarities of a particular processor architecture. The relationship between the hardware components of such a typical system is illustrated in Fig. 7.1. Central to the system is the hardware 'bus'; the bus provides the electronic connections between the other system components. It specifies the hardware protocols that are to be used to exchange information and to synchronise the operation of the other hardware components. A number of standard bus configurations are commercially available, together with compatible families of processors and peripheral devices.

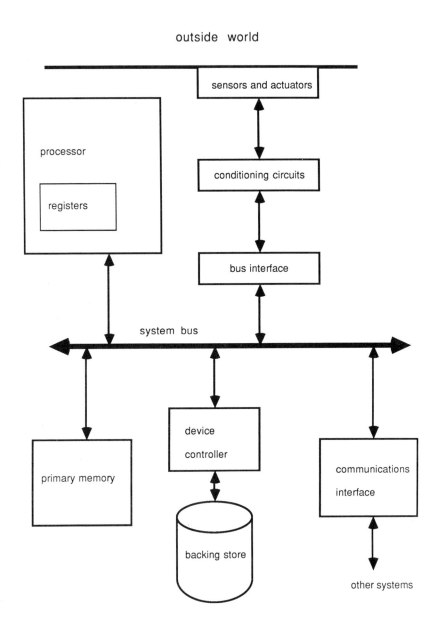

Fig 7.1 - Hardware components of a computer system

The dominant system component is the processor; it is the active component which does the work and executes the programs. The processor controls and coordinates the operation of the other components of the system. Intimately associated with the processor is the primary memory which contains both the programs that are to be executed and the data to be manipulated, both in encoded form. The organisation of the memory was introduced in Chapter 1; it will be considered further in the next section which examines some low-level processor features and memory access methods.

The processor can easily access the data and programs that are contained in the primary memory. However, the memory is limited, and the information may be lost when the system is switched off. Most systems provide for the long-term storage of information on some magnetic medium such as disks or tapes. These devices maintain data in large blocks, typically containing 512 bytes or more. To access data from backing store, the processor must first arrange for the correct block of data to be copied into the primary memory before the individual data elements can become accessible to it.

The interface between the computer system and the outside world is provided by the peripheral devices. These devices may either communicate with a human operator using typed or printed words, or graphical displays, or they may communicate with the environment or other machinery using sensors and actuators. The data that is to be communicated must undergo a transformation between the binary representation that is used within the computer system and the external manifestations of the data, such as character strings, voltages or temperatures. These transformations are performed by specialised conditioning circuits; the peripheral devices may exchange information in its digital form using a fairly standard interface to the system's bus. The final system component is the communications interface which provides the connection to other computer systems, and is covered in the next chapter.

The remainder of this chapter is composed of three parts: the first section examines the structure of the processor and the primary memory, and their relationship to software processes; the second section introduces the architecture of the hardware interface to peripheral devices; the final section examines the structure of the interface between a software process and the hardware of a peripheral device.

7.2. PROCESSORS AND PROCESSES

The primary memory of the computer system is used to store the program instructions and data, encoded as binary numbers. The memory is composed of a series of 'words'. Each word of memory is identified by a unique 'address'; the number of bits used to specify this address limits the potential 'address space' of the system. On very small systems, such as those intended for simple process control applications, the address space may only extend to a few thousand locations; however, processors based on VLSI families of chips have address spaces of several million words or more. The address space defines the maximum possible memory of the system, although in practice only a subset of the addresses may have corresponding physical memory locations; attempts to access addresses that do not have physical implementations result in the erroneous behaviour of the program.

Each word contains an ordered set of independent 'bits' which may take a logical value of true or false; alternatively they may be considered to take a numeric value of zero or one. The patterns of values of the bits may be used to represent program instructions or data values. The method of encoding program instructions into binary patterns is determined by the processor hardware. There are several conventions for the representation within the memory of other data, such as integers, real numbers and characters. The processor's basic instructions that manipulate data assume that the data is represented using certain of these conventions. However, other hardware components may use different conventions of data representation, and the processor may be required to translate between these representations to communicate with these devices.

Microprocessor based systems tend to use a word size of 16 or 32 bits, so each word can also be considered to be composed of a number of 'bytes', where a byte is composed of 8 bits. Bytes can encode 256 values and are commonly used to encode alphanumeric characters using ASCII (American Standard Code for Information Interchange) standard. This is convenient since the majority of terminals and printing devices now use ASCII coding, so data may be transferred directly between the processor and the peripheral devices. However, some processors use different sized words and employ different character coding schemes; these schemes often use fewer bits per character to represent a restricted character set. In such cases it may be necessary for the processor to perform a translation between the internal coding and ASCII coding when information is being exchanged with an interface device.

Similar problems of incompatible representations of data are sometimes encountered when interfacing to analog-to-digital converters. Some devices use fewer bits than the processor uses to represent a number; this is because the restricted resolution of the device can distinguish only a small number of distinct voltage levels which, typically, can be represented using twelve bits. Another problem of representation may be encountered in the method used to encode binary numbers, especially when negative numbers are involved; in which case suitable transformations will have to be performed by the processor before the data can be manipulated in numerical calculations.

In addition to the memory, the processor itself usually contains a number of registers that are used for the short-term storage of information. Some registers have a specific purpose; for example, most processors have a particular register, the program counter or PC, which is used to identify which is the next instruction to be executed. Other general purpose registers can be used to store data values to be used in numerical calculations, or to hold addresses of significant memory locations. In general, data held within a register can be accessed more rapidly by the processor than data that is held in memory.   Also, the processor can often apply a wider range of operations to the contents of registers than to the contents of memory locations, and it has a wider range of uses to which it can put data once it is held in a register.

7.2.1. Data manipulation instructions

The basic range of operations that a processor can be programmed to perform is called its 'instruction set'.   This usually runs to many tens, if not hundreds of different instructions; however, most of them fall into a few groups of related instructions.

The group of instructions which provides arithmetic and logical operations on data values often accounts for a large proportion of the instruction set, although these instructions may not account for as high a proportion of the instructions executed. The details of these instructions are of interest to a programmer implementing a compiler, but they have little impact upon the implementation of processes, or upon the structure of the operating system.

The instructions which effect calculations on data are supplemented by a number of instructions which move data within the computer. These load information from memory into registers; move it between registers; store it back into memory from a register; or move it directly from one memory location to another.

The lowest level of representation of a program that is used by a programmer is usually expressed in the processor's assembler code; it is also used by high-level language compilers which often translate their input programs into equivalent programs in assembler code. An assembler code program consists of a direct representation of each machine level instruction in a slightly more humanly comprehensible form than the actual binary coding used by the processor. The executable form of the program is produced from the assembler code by first translating the assembler code program into a binary form using an 'assembler program', and then linking the program together with the code of standard library functions using a 'linkage editor' or 'linker program'.

An assembler code instruction consists of a mnemonic 'op-code' which identifies the instruction to be executed, followed by suitable 'operands'. Operands are analogous to a procedure's parameters; they must specify suitable data to be operated upon during the execution of the instruction. Operands usually have one of three forms: i) simple constant values that are encoded directly into the instruction; ii) the name of a register that is to be manipulated using some naming schemes such as A, B, C or R1, R2, R3 etc.; iii) a memory address.

A processor may have a number of 'addressing modes' that are used to specify the memory address to be used by an instruction. The most direct mode is 'absolute addressing', when the actual memory address is incorporated directly into the instruction.   When expressed in assembler code, absolute addresses are usually replaced by symbolic names or labels to make the program more readable. For example, an assembler code instruction to add a constant value of one to the number held in the memory location called *spaces* might take the form:-

    add   *1*   *spaces*

However, this mechanism is often restricted to addressing only a subset of the full address space. It is also a very inflexible mechanism since the program always addresses the same memory locations. Most instruction sets allow these operand addresses to be expressed as offsets relative to an address contained in a processor register; this provides a direct implementation of the block-structured addressing mechanisms discussed in section 1.2.6. For example, if the program is organised so that a register, say R1, always points to the variables allocated in the current block of a high-level language, then if the variable *space* is known to be the third variable in the block it might be incremented using an instruction of the form:-

    add   *1*   *3 (R1)*

The processor architecture usually imposes some constraints on the size of the offset that can be used, as well as only allowing a subset of the full set of registers to be used for address calculations. At any point in a program's execution, the extent of the accessible memory addresses is determined by the contents of registers that can be used for addressing purposes.

The concept of a stack was also introduced in section 1.2.6; some processors incorporate the concept directly into their instruction set, and either provide a dedicated 'stack-pointer' register, (SP), or assume that a particular general purpose register will be used for this function. The processor would normally supply instructions such as **push** and **pop** to transfer data between working registers and the top of the stack. For example, the following program adds together the top two items on the stack and replaces them with their sum, assuming that the values must be moved into working registers before they can be added:-

    pop   *R2*
    pop   *R3*
    add   *R2*   *R3*
    push   *R3*

When a stack is provided, it is often used by some other instructions, which are considered later in this chapter.

Processors designed to support the provision of multiple software processes often contain special 'memory-management' hardware which restricts a process' access to the memory in addition to any restrictions that are imposed by the addressing modes. The aim of the memory management unit (MMU) is to prevent a process accessing or corrupting the private data of another process. MMUs usually provide each software process with a restricted logical address space which is mapped onto part of the physical

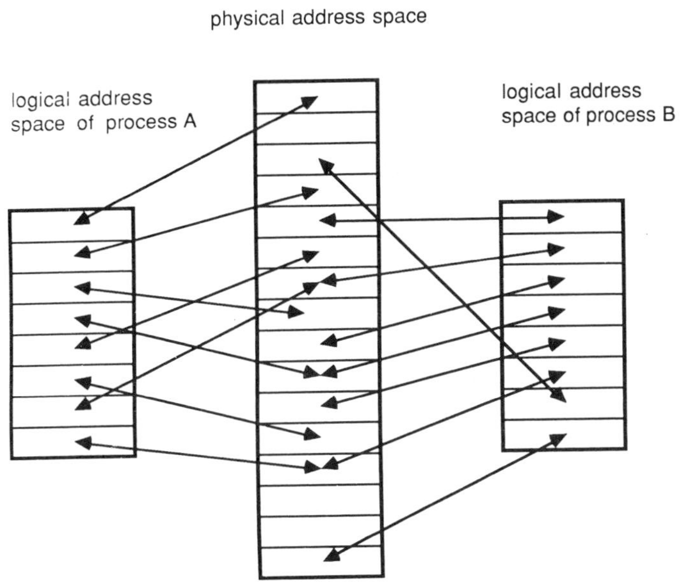

physical address space

logical address
space of process A

logical address
space of process B

Fig. 7.2. - Logical operation of a Memory Management Unit.

memory. The MMU contains two sets of registers which are used to contain the base addresses and sizes of segments of real memory that are allocated to the current active process, the process is prevented from accessing any other memory locations that fall outside of this space. Other processes can be allocated to other memory locations by loading the registers of the MMU with different values, the operation of the MMU is illustrated in Fig. 7.2. Normal processes are unable to change the MMU's registers and are restricted to accessing their designated memory area; however, the mapping can be changed by the processor when it is acting in its 'supervisory' or 'kernel' mode, which is discussed later in this section.

7.2.2. The flow of control

In addition to instructions which manipulate data, the processor must also provide some instructions to change the sequence of execution of instructions. By default, the program counter (PC) is incremented each time it is used to fetch an instruction from memory to be executed; this results in the sequential execution of a series of instructions. The order may be changed by **jump** or **branch** instructions which specify the address of the next instruction that is to be executed. Program loops can be produced by jumping back to an instruction at a lower memory address; for example, the following program would run indefinitely:-

> *label:*   *<instruction_1>*
>   *<instruction_2>*
>   **jump**   *label*

To provide more flexible operations, the processor must also implement some form of **conditional jump** instructions which change the flow of control only if some condition holds within the execution of a process. The current trend is for the processor to use a special status register (the processor status register or PSR) to record its status; it is this register which is tested by these instructions. Each bit of the PSR records information about some aspect of the processor's status, the individual bits are set or cleared as a by-product of the execution of instructions.   Each bit can also be explicitly set, cleared, or tested by the action of specific instructions. For example, most processors have a *zero* flag, which is set to true when the execution of an arithmetic instruction results in the value of zero, otherwise the flag is set to false. A compiler might transform the following program loop:-

> **repeat**
>   *<body-of-loop>*
> **until** *x=10*

into an assembler code program that tests the *zero* flag:-

> *again:*
>   *<body-of-loop>*
>   **move**   *x*   *R3*
>   **sub**   *10*   *R3*
>   **jump if zero not set**   *again*

Other common flags associated with arithmetic operations indicate if their result was negative, or if they produced an arithmetic overflow. Some other flags intimately associated with the processor's internal status are often included in the PSR; these flags are considered later in this chapter.

Processors usually provide some hardware support for procedure calls. The transfer of control is more complex in a procedure call than a simple jump instruction since the processor will need to be able to continue executing the instructions that follow the procedure call instruction after it has completed executing the procedure. The processor needs to save a 'return address' which it uses to jump from the end of the procedure back to the calling program. This return address is usually simply the value of the program counter, PC. To enable nested or recursive procedure calls to be made, the processor usually provides a **procedure call** instruction which saves the return address on the stack; there is a complementary **procedure exit** instruction which pops this destination address from the stack.

On entering a procedure, one of the first duties of a process is to save the contents of any of the processor's registers that will be used during the procedure's execution. These operations are usually programmed automatically by the compiler, which generates code to push the registers onto the process' stack. Before exiting the procedure the process restores the values of its registers by popping them from the stack. This means that the calling procedure need not be concerned about side-effects of the operation of the called procedure. For example, the code of a procedure that uses three working registers would take the form:-

proc-1:

```
push    R1
push    R2
push    R3
<body_of_code>
pop     R3
pop     R2
pop     R1
procedure exit
```

The *<body_of_code>* can use the three working registers that have been saved on the stack; it can also use the stack provided that any temporary results are removed before the final sequence of instructions that restore the registers is encountered.   In this way the **procedure exit** instruction should find the return address at the top of the stack. Notice that it is quite possible for the *<body_of_code>* to contain calls to other procedures, or even to itself, provided that they restore the registers and the stack to their former conditions after the call.

In practice, it is possible for each process to use a single stack for several functions, such as:

(1)   to save the process context on a procedure call;

(2)   to allocate local variables in a block structured language;

(3)   to save temporary results during the evaluation of expressions;

(4)   to pass parameters to a procedure by placing them on the stack before the procedure is called.

The resulting stack is illustrated in Fig. 7.3; obviously, the details of the stack structure vary with both the processor and the conventions adopted by the language compiler that is used to generate the code.

7.2.3. The kernel

The previous section outlined the structure of application processes within the memory of a multi-user computer system. In order to enhance the security of the system, these processes were prevented from performing some critical

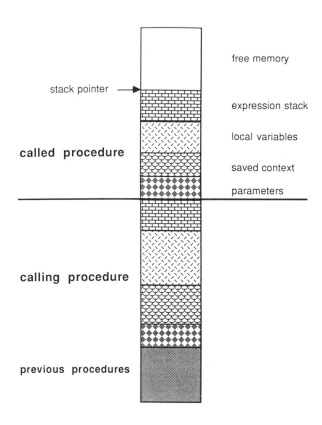

Fig. 7.3. - The organisation of a typical stack.

operations, such as manipulating the registers of a memory management unit. There are usually a number of such 'privileged instructions' that concern the basic operation of the processor and other shared resources, such as peripheral devices. These privileged instructions can be executed only when the machine is in a privileged state. In order to enforce the overall integrity of the software system, the promotion of processes to this privileged state is strictly controlled.

The implementation of most computer systems is based on the concept of a 'kernel' or 'supervisor' module that provides a collection of fundamental routines to control and to coordinate the operation of the constituent software processes. These kernel routines are executed with the processor in its privileged state and can therefore perform operations such as controlling the memory management unit. Kernels also provide the high-level functions of the system, such as the multiplexing of application processes onto the processor and the implementation of the inter-process communication and synchronisation.

The precise set of operations that are provided by a kernel will depend on the process coordination model that it was designed to support. A kernel designed to support monitor-based interaction will provide operations to acquire and release exclusive access to areas of memory and to send and receive signals. In contrast, a kernel designed for message passing is unlikely to provide these functions but instead it will support the sending, receiving, and buffering of messages.

An application process can invoke the execution of a kernel operation in a similar manner to calling one of its own procedures; however, there are significant differences. Kernel routines are entered not by using the procedure call mechanism but by **trap** or **interrupt** instructions which are more complex in their operation. The trap mechanism not only changes the sequence of instructions that are to be executed, but also changes the addressing context to that of the kernel, and promotes the process to the privileged mode. Like the procedure call mechanism, the trap mechanism must save enough of the process' context to allow it to be resumed at some later stage by a complementary **return from trap** instruction. This means that, in addition to the values of the processor's general registers, the value of the PSR (processor status register) and values of the registers of the memory management unit, need to be saved and later restored.

The kernel routines do not form part of the application process' address space; they reside in a separate memory area and can be used by all application processes. The **trap** instruction does not specify the address of the routine to be executed; instead, it provides a code indicating the desired action. The processor uses the code as an index to a table of 'trap vectors' which is located in some predefined memory area; the elements of this table contain the actual addresses of the procedures. This organisation is illustrated in Fig. 7.4. The table of vectors provides the interface between the application processes and the kernel. Provided that the table contains the correct addresses, the organisation of the code of the kernel routines can be changed without affecting the application processes. The vector table forms part of the kernel, not the application program. This arrangement ensures the independence of the structure of the application processes and the structure of the kernel.

The kernel is also responsible for multiplexing the processes onto the processor. An application process may not be resumed immediately after it has requested the execution of a kernel operation; for example, the operation may involve some delay, such as waiting for a message. The kernel may choose to suspend the operation of the process and instead resume the

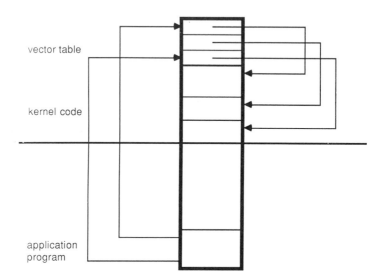

Fig. 7.4. - The interface to the kernel.

operation of another process which had be delayed during a previous kernel operation. However, provided that there are no critical timing constraints, the processes should be unaware that this multiplexing is being performed.

There is considerable variety in the size and complexity of kernels, depending on their intended area of application. Kernels of large, general purpose, multi-tasking operating systems often consist of tens or hundreds of kilobytes of code and provide extensive facilities. These kernels are often written in a high-level, possibly concurrent, language and may interface to a smaller inner kernel. At the other extreme, a small process-control application may interface to a minimal kernel of a few hundred bytes which simply provides the processor multiplexing operations.

The kernel usually provides the interface between the application program and the peripheral devices. The nature of the software interface is examined in the final section of the chapter, after the hardware interface has been introduced.

7.3. HARDWARE INTERFACE TO PERIPHERAL DEVICES

One of the least standardised and least integrated aspects of computer architecture is the interface to peripheral devices. Differences may arise between
the treatment of different types of device by a single system, and between the
way in which similar devices are handled on different systems. However, the
differences tend to lie at the level of implementation detail or in peculiarities
of the algorithm needed to drive a particular device, rather than in differences
of fundamental principle.

The difficulties of driving peripheral devices arise because the operation
of each device involves the coordination of at least two processes: a software
process that is implemented by the computer system's processor, and a process that is implemented by the hardware of the peripheral device itself in
combination wtih the external environment in which it operates (see Fig. 7.5).
Difficulties arise for the programmer of the software process if the external
process is poorly or incompletely defined or if it exhibits time dependent
behaviour. Since the external process is usually already established, any
adaptation or accommodation that is required in order that the two processes
can cooperate is expected to be provided by the software process.

The hardware interface between the processor and the peripheral device
is usually predefined and inflexible. The interface must enable the processor
to pass commands to the peripheral device to initiate actions, and for the peripheral device to return information about its status to the processor. Most
devices also need to exchange data with the process, passing it inwards from
the environment, for example from a keyboard or sensor device, or outwards,
for example to a display, or in both directions, as in the case of a disk drive.
Peripheral devices usually provide at least two registers through which these
different forms of information are exchanged: a command register for commands and status reports, and a data register. Some more complex devices
require several command registers to be initialised to define their operation.

Processors usually employ one of the two common schemes to access
the registers of peripheral devices: 'port addressing' and 'memory mapping'.
In the 'port addressing' scheme each peripheral register has a unique
identifier, or port address. The processor uses special instructions, such as **in**
or **out,** which transfer information between a specified processor register and
the specified port, e.g.

> **in**   *port_1   R1*

and

> **out**   *R3   port_2*

With the port-addressing scheme, it is possible to retain a tight control
over the access to all peripheral devices by restricting the possible methods of
communication with a peripheral device to these privileged instructions. The
disadvantage of the port addressing method is the overhead of always having
to use one of the processor's registers as an intermediary between a software

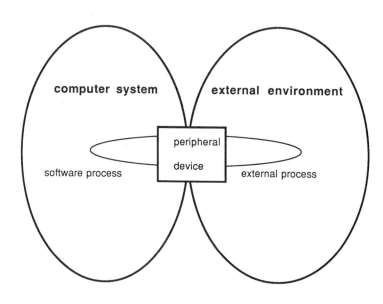

Fig 7.5. - Peripheral handling regarded as two processes.

process and the device; this means that interaction with the device may require more instructions than are needed in the 'memory mapped' scheme.

In the 'memory mapped' scheme device registers are inserted into the processor's address space, in place of some some memory locations. When the processor accesses a memory address that has been mapped onto a device register, it operates on the contents of the register and exchanges information with the device, not with the memory. The processor itself is not aware of the mapping and it simply accesses the device using any of the mechanisms available for accessing memory locations; in contrast to the 'port addressing' scheme, no special instructions are required. If a device register is mapped onto the location identified by the label *printout*, the data could be transferred to the device using an instruction of the form:-

move   *R3*   *printout*

In this scheme, the control of access to peripheral devices can be enforced by the memory management unit. The system programmer can ensure that the memory addresses of the device registers never form part of the address space of a non-privileged process. This ensures that a process would have to enter the kernel to gain access to the memory area containing the registers, and it allows their access to be monitored. The interface of peripheral devices using memory mapping requires more hardware logic associated with each device since memory addresses are usually specified using more bits than are used for port addresses. Because this logic lies in the peripheral interface, a processor designed for 'port addressing' can be used in a system with memory mapped peripherals. For example, the Intel 8086 family of processors provide a port addressing scheme, but the IBM-PC computer, which is based on these chips, uses memory mapping. The converse may not true; a processor that is designed for use with memory mapped peripherals may lack the basic instructions needed for port addressing.

7.3.1. Interacting with typical devices

Both modes of addressing peripheral devices employ the same basic pattern of interaction between the processor and a device; the differences lie only in the details of the instructions used. The details of the interface between peripheral devices and processors is one of the least standardised and most poorly defined aspects of computer systems. The following two descriptions give idealised accounts of the way in which a processor could interface to a simple printer and to a keyboard device. In practice, there are many more detailed problems involved in controlling such devices, many of which will not even be documented in the manufacturer's technical publications. In addition to their control registers, both devices will require a buffer register through which data will be exchanged with the processor, one character at a time.

To output a character to the printer, the processor simply inserts it into the buffer register; the device control logic detects that the buffer has been accessed and it initiates the transfer of the character to the printer. There is a considerable difference between the speed of operation of the processor and that of the peripheral device; the processor may execute tens or even hundreds of thousands of instructions in the time it takes to print a single character. Therefore, the processor must be prevented from requesting the printing of another character until the current one has been dealt with. The printer's status register allows this synchronisation.

The status register is a set of independent bits or flags; some are under the control of the device, some are under the control of the processor, others can be affected by both parties. A simple device like a printer may have only three or four flags defined; only two of these will be introduced immediately, the *busy* and the *done* flags. When the printer receives the character for printing it sets its *busy* flag to true, indicating to the processor that it is not ready to receive any more characters. If the processor inserts any characters into the buffer register while the *busy* flag is set, they will simply be ignored; therefore, the processor should check the condition of the status register before inserting data into the buffer register. When the interface logic has output the character and is ready for the next one, it clears the *busy* flag and sets the *done* flag. The processor can detect this change of state by repeatedly testing the status register; it can then send the next character to be output to the printer interface. Inserting the next character in the buffer will reset the *done* flag and set the *busy* flag again. When there are no characters to be output, the printer control logic simply remains in an idle state waiting for the next request.

The operation of the printer is illustrated in Fig. 7.6. It can be viewed as the interaction of two processes communicating through buffers; one process is implemented by the interface logic of the peripheral device, and the other by software running on the processor. Chapter 2 introduced a number of the synchronisation problems associated with shared buffers. Most of these problems are solved in this case by the use of special hardware logic which provides the indivisible updating of the buffer register and status flags. The synchronisation required to prevent buffer underflow is implemented in the hardware logic, which causes the interface to remain idle when there is no character to be output. However, the synchronisation required to prevent the overflow of the buffer must be implemented in the software routine that

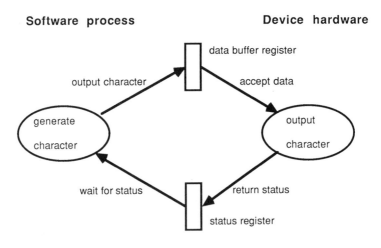

Fig. 7.6. - Peripheral handling seen as buffered communication.

checks the condition of the status register before accessing the buffer register.

The interface to a keyboard can be structured in a manner complementary to that of the printer interface; the significant difference here is that the rate of production of information is determined by the environment external to the computer system and it is not under the computer's control. This is, therefore, a 'real-time' system in which the timing constraints are externally imposed upon the computer system. Three flags will be considered here initially, *busy*, *done* and *error*. The input of a single character from a keyboard takes a long time on the processor's time-scale. When the interface logic detects that a character is being input, it sets the *busy* flag in the status register. When the character has been successfully received, it is deposited in the buffer register and the *done* flag is set. If the processor is monitoring the *done* flag, it can detect the arrival of the character which can then be extracted from the buffer register. Accessing the buffer register causes the hardware logic in the interface to reset the *busy* and *done* flags.

If the processor is not monitoring the status register, it may be slow in responding to the setting of the *done* flag, and another character may arrive before the buffer has been reset. In this case the interface logic will simply discard the new character and set the *error* flag in the status register. The software process is responsible for monitoring the *error* flag and instigating any corrective action when it is set, such as sending an error report to the output device associated with the keyboard. In order to avoid such errors, the processor needs to examine the status register at a more frequent rate than the fastest rate at which characters may be input. This policy of repeated inspection, or polling, is usually a waste of effort since no input will have arrived since the register was previously examined. Furthermore, if the processor has a large number of input devices that require monitoring and servicing, it may be difficult to ensure that the registers of the faster devices are examined at an adequate rate.

7.3.2. Interrupts

The problem of ensuring that the processor will have an adequately rapid response to the operation of a peripheral device without wasting too much of its time polling is usually solved by the hardware logic of the interrupt system. Instead of passively waiting for the processor to recognise a change in the state of its status register, a device equipped with an interrupt system may force the processor to perform a context switch to the software process responsible for the particular device interface. This software process is called the 'device handler' or 'interrupt service routine'.

When a device has completed its interaction with the external environment and requires the attention of the processor, it sends a special hardware signal, an interrupt request, to the processor. For example, when the printer interface completes the transmission of a character and sets its *done* flag, it will also cause an interrupt, similarly, the keyboard interface will generate an interrupt when it receives a character and sets its *done* flag. Whenever the processor completes an instruction, its hardware examines the status of the interrupt request signals from all of the peripheral devices. This test is virtually instantaneous since it is implemented directly in the processor's hardware. If there are no outstanding requests the processor simply proceeds with its next instruction in its current process context. If there is an outstanding interrupt request then an interrupt sequence is initiated. This involves:-

(1)   Saving the state of the current process.

(2)   Identifying the interrupting device.

(3)   Locating the correct service routine, and loading the associated process context into the processor's registers.

The processor is now in the correct state to service the interrupting device and it can retrieve input data from the registers of the input device or it can provide additional data for output devices. The operation of the peripheral device can then be resumed. The interrupt service routine may then have to perform various 'housekeeping' functions, such as storing input data into a software buffer and communicating to other processes the fact that the data has arrived. Once these operations have been completed, the context of the interrupted process is retrieved and reloaded into the processor; the interrupted process is then resumed at its next instruction as if nothing had happened.

Processors provide varying levels of support for the operations involved in changing to the correct context to service a device. Any aspects that are not provided by the hardware have to be implemented by the underlying software. Like a **trap** instruction, a hardware interrupt causes the processor to save the value of the program counter, and possibly the values of some other registers, and to begin executing instructions at a particular memory location determined by the hardware. The system's programmer must arrange for the interrupt service routine to be loaded into this address. The first duty of this routine is to save the contents of any registers that are not automatically saved by the hardware.

In the most primitive interrupt systems, all interrupts cause the processor to jump to the same memory address. The process must then poll the status register of each device in order to identify which one caused the interrupt; the process can then jump to the appropriate service routine. More sophisticated hardware may cause the processor to jump directly to a different address for each device and enter the correct interrupt service routine directly.

To simplify the programming of interrupt service routines, the hardware usually inhibits the effect of further interrupts once the processor responds to an interrupt. Otherwise the processor might be interrupted part of the way through changing between process contexts, which could result in chaos.

The interrupted process is later resumed using a **return from interrupt** instruction which reverses the context saving operations that were performed automatically when an interrupt was detected; the instruction then re-enables interrupts once a coherent context is established.

Inhibiting the effects of interrupts from all devices while a processor is executing an interrupt service routine can cause problems on systems with very fast input devices, since the devices will lose data if they are not serviced rapidly enough. Most hardware systems provide instructions to re-enable or inhibit interrupts; once an interrupt service routine has been fully entered, it is common practice to re-enable interrupts. Interrupts may need to be inhibited again at the end of the service routine to ensure the smooth resumption of the interrupted context. While interrupts are re-enabled, the interrupt service routine itself is vulnerable to interruption and can become suspended while another routine is invoked to service a different device. Like other interrupted processes it is resumed later, after the interrupting device has been serviced. The hardware of the interrupt system usually provides a prioritisation system which prevents low priority devices from interrupting the service routine of higher priority devices. For example, the priority scheme might allow a keyboard interrupt to suspend the execution of printer output routine but not to suspend the execution of a disk drive service routine.

As well as being able to enable or disable the entire interrupt system, a program can usually prohibit interrupts from each individual device. The device status register usually contains an *interrupt enable* flag (or an *interrupt inhibit* flag) which is under the control of the processor. This means that a device can be prohibited from interrupting its own interrupt service routine, and that an unused device can be prohibited from generating spurious interrupts.

Because interrupt service routines can pre-empt the normal processes, their operation may disturb the overall scheduling policy of the system. To minimise the disturbance caused by peripheral device operations, the usual practice is to perform the minimum possible operations within the service routine and to implement as much of the control algorithm as possible as a normal process. Thus, device-driving software usually takes the form of two loosely coupled asynchronous processes which communicate through a cyclic buffer. The details of this structure are usually hidden from the application program, since they are implemented within the kernel and are accessed through the standard kernel interface.

For example, an application program might access a printing device by repeatedly calling a *print_character* routine within the kernel. It would specify the character that is to be printed by using some established protocol for parameter passing, such as placing the character in a particular register, or pushing it onto the stack. The kernel routine would retrieve the parameter, insert it into a buffer associated with the printer and update the counter variables of the buffer. This would complete the execution of the kernel routine and control would be returned to the application program.

When the printer completes the output of a character it generates an interrupt and its service routine is executed. This routine examines the cyclic buffer of characters waiting to be printed. If characters are available then the routine extracts the next character and updates the counter variables. The interrupt service routine then deposits the character that is to be printed into the device register, which initiates the printer hardware cycle. The interrupt service routine then relinquishes its use of the processor and the interrupted process is resumed. When the printer hardware has output the character, it generates another interrupt and the service routine is despatched to extract another character from the cyclic buffer. If the buffer is empty the service routine simply resets the printer interface and then exits.

If the application program uses a kernel routine to print a character and finds that the buffer has been emptied, it invokes an operation to restart the printer. On the other hand, if it finds that the buffer is full, its operation is delayed until the printer service routine generates some space in the buffer and signals to the kernel routine that it may resume its operation.

Access to the keyboard input would be implemented in a similar manner. The interrupt service routine would extract the character from the device buffer; this operation resets the keyboard interface ready for the next input. The service routine then deposits the character into a cyclic buffer, or discards the character if the buffer is full and reports the error to the user. The application program extracts the characters from the buffer by calling a kernel routine. If the application issues a request for characters when the input buffer is empty, its kernel routine is usually delayed until some input becomes available.

Programming the routines to access the cyclic buffers requires special care since mutual exclusion of access to the buffer variables is not enforced. It is quite possible for an application program to be accessing a buffer when the device that uses the same buffer generates an interrupt. Control is then passed to the interrupt service routine, which then manipulates the buffer variables before returning control to the application program. Fortunately, the application program cannot pre-empt the interrupt service routine. The programmer must exercise great care over the order in which variables are accessed and updated within these routines. He must also ensure that any variables that have the potential to be accessed by both processes are updated using indivisible machine level instructions that act directly on the contents of the memory location; the processes must not keep local copies of these shared values in the registers of the processor since these values may become outdated. As a last resort it is usually possible for the application program to inhibit interrupts while it accesses the buffer and then to re-enable them once it has finished updating the variables. However, this technique should be avoided if at all possible, since it will inhibit the operation of all the peripheral devices controlled be the processor.

7.3.3. Direct memory access devices - DMA

The previous examples have dealt with simple devices which operate on single data items and which access only their own hardware buffers. Such devices require a good deal of attention from the processor to transmit each data item, but their slow rate of operation means that this does not generate too significant a load. However, the processing load to control fast, bulk transfer devices, such as disk drives or fast communications interfaces, could become significant. Therefore, these devices are usually provided with more sophisticated control logic which enables them to transfer blocks of data directly between the device and the processor's memory with the minimum of attention from the processor. Such devices have 'direct memory access' and have DMA controllers.

The principle of DMA device operation is similar to that of ordinary character-oriented devices. The processor must first establish the correct values in the controller's registers, which are accessed in the usual manner. However, instead of depositing the data value to be transmitted in the data register, the processor provides a memory address indicating either where the data is to be found for an output operation, or where it is to be deposited for an input operation. The processor must also set the contents of a counter register to contain the number of items of data that are to be transferred. In the case of a disk controller, the processor must also initialise another register to indicate the location on the disk that is to be accessed. Once these parameters have been set the processor can send a *start* command to the controller, either by executing a special instruction or by setting a bit in the status register. The controller then performs the transfer of the specified number of data items directly between a contiguous series of memory locations and the peripheral device, at a very high speed. The controller generates an interrupt only when it has completed the entire operation or if it encounters some error, such as an unreadable area of disk.

DMA controllers are usually used to handle blocks of at least 512 bytes at a time, thus saving a considerable amount of processor activity. However, since DMA controllers access the same memory as the processor, they may reduce its rate of processing when there is contention for access to the memory. DMA devices need to be programmed more carefully than simple devices since they introduce genuine concurrent access to memory locations.

7.4. ACCESSING DEVICES FROM HIGH-LEVEL LANGUAGES

Most general purpose programming languages do not provide facilities for accessing the computer hardware; their aim is the hide the machine-dependent details as much as possible. Most programming languages do not incorporate the concept of there being a range of peripheral devices; interaction with their external environment is usually provided by standard procedures which operate on external files. The underlying operating system is relied upon to implement the concept of a file and to implement a uniform interface between the program and the various peripheral devices. Usually the aim of the operating system is to hide any device-dependent features and present the application program with a uniform interface to a file-system. Although this approach is suitable for the majority of applications, it is not appropriate for the growing number of control-oriented applications or for the implementation of operating systems themselves.

The early real-time oriented high-level languages such as Coral-66 (Woodward, 1970) and RTL/2 (Barnes, 1976) recognised both the benefits of high-level language features and the need for access to low level features. The designers of these languages adopted the pragmatic approach that, since features for direct access to the machine would be used only rarely, the language would provide only the minimum of such support. The approach adopted in the design of these languages is to allow segments of assembler code to be incorporated into the program. This provides total flexibility for the skilled programmer, but it reduces the security and integrity of the program since the assembler coded segments may violate the language rules that the compiler attempts to enforce. The approach also results in programs that contain both machine-dependent and compiler-dependent features, since the assembler code segments will have to be designed to interface with the particular conventions of the code produced by the compiler.

More recent languages, such as Modula (Wirth, 1977a), have attempted to overcome these problems by incorporating device access and interrupt handling directly into a high-level language. The implementation of these particular aspects of the language were changed in the revision to Modula-2; however, since the original features map more directly onto the concepts developed in this chapter they will still be used here for illustration. The features provided by Modula have since been adopted and refined in Ada. Features must be provided to specify two aspects of processor-device interaction:-

1) The location and format of device registers.
2) Interrupt handling and synchronisation with other tasks.

7.4.1. Accessing device registers

Access to memory mapped device registers from a high-level language is quite simple since they can be treated like program variables. The programmer simply declares within the program some variables which are to used to represent the device registers, together with clauses which specify the absolute memory addresses to be used. The addresses are usually expressed in octal notation to match most hardware documentation. The data type of the variable used to represent the data register of the device must be declared to match the form of data handled by the device; for example, a keyboard input register would be declared as a character variable. In Modula this may be expressed as:-

    var

        keyb_data_reg [177560B]: char;

Modula provides a primitive data type, *bits*, which implements an array of boolean variables packed into one word which can be used to describe a device status register. Each individual flag in the register can be accessed using the array subscript notation, e.g.

if *keyb_status_reg[2]* then ...

Devices sometimes use groups of bits within a register to represent binary numbers. For example, if a disk-drive controller could have eight attached drives, three bits of the status register would be needed to encode the identity of the drive to be accessed. Unfortunately, this is very inconvenient to express using Modula. This problem has been overcome in Ada which allows a record structure to be used to represent a status register, and allows the programmer to specify the mapping between the field names and the bits in the memory. These mechanisms allow memory mapped device registers to be manipulated within a program using all the facilities that are available for accessing variables, so the registers may be used directly in conditional clauses or assignment statements to test or change their values.

Unfortunately, these mechanisms cannot be used with port-addressed peripherals which are accessed using special machine-level instructions. Modula makes no provision for accessing these devices; Ada merely specifies that the compiler and run-time system should provide the implementation-dependent procedures, *send_control* and *receive_control*, to communicate with them.

7.4.2. Interrupt handling

Section 7.3.2 introduced the concept of an interrupt service routine that acts as an intermediary between application processes and the hardware of the peripheral device. In many cases it is possible to consider the joint operation of the peripheral device and its service routine as a single cyclic process implemented in two parts. One part is implemented by the processor when it executes the code of the interrupt service routine, and the second part is implemented directly by the hardware of the peripheral device. This view of device interfacing was adopted in Modula where interfaces to peripheral devices are encapsulated in **device module** definitions. The language features that are provided to access the processor and peripheral device hardware are confined to these enhanced modules. Modula programs are usually structured with a simple **device process** to service each peripheral device, usually using the buffering techniques outlined earlier in this chapter. Each module contains a buffer area, procedures that are used by the other program modules to access the buffer, and a 'device process' which acts as the interrupt service routine. The program in Fig. 7.7 illustrates the structure of an interface to the idealised printer device described earlier in this chapter. Some detailed program examples using Modula to interface to the peripheral devices of a PDP-11 computer are given in one of the original papers by Wirth (1977b). The buffering allows the other processes in the system to proceed asynchronously and independently of the operation of the peripheral devices. Any synchronisation between the device processes and their customer processes can be implemented using Modula's standard *signal* mechanisms.

device modules contain several special features that relate to the hardware architecture of the processor. The heading of the module must define the hardware priority of the peripheral device that it serves. The device process itself must define the interrupt vector address of the device that it services. It must also contain the variable definitions that specify the device registers and their memory addresses so that it can exchange information with the device and control its operation. The device process can use the special procedure *doio* to synchronise its operation with the operation of a hardware device. The process becomes suspended when it executes the *doio* statement and is resumed when its associated device generates an interrupt. This is very similar to Modula's standard synchronisation technique of waiting for a *signal* from another process.

In Ada, the standard interprocess communication and synchronisation mechanisms are provided by the rendezvous, which is also used to interface the hardware processes of peripheral devices to their interrupt service routines. The data buffering and device-control functions can be implemented in one task which provides two **entrys**. One **entry** provides a standard interface for the other tasks in the program. Application tasks rendezvous with the peripheral-controller task, which either accepts data destined to be output and inserts it into a local buffer, or retrieves incoming data from a buffer and delivers it to the application task.

The other **entry** provides the interrupt service routine, and must specify the interrupt address of the device it serves. In effect, an interrupt from the device calls this **entry** which will be serviced when the handler task next **accepts** a call to the **entry**. During the rendezvous, the process must transfer data between the device and the software buffer and perform any necessary operations on the device status register. This mechanism allows the control of devices to be integrated into an application program in a coherent manner that is consistent with general structure of Ada programs.

7.4.3. Peripheral interfacing and message systems

Communication between processes and peripheral devices can easily be modelled at a language level using message passing techniques; a process can simply use **send** and **receive** primitives addressed to the device. However, the message passing primitives are quite high-level constructs compared to the machine level operations that are needed to interface to a peripheral device, so extensive low-level support is required. This is particularly true of asynchronous message systems which need the support of underlying message buffering software. Typically these systems would interface to a kernel system which handles inter-process communication and interrupt handling.

```
device module printer[5]; {hardware priority of printer}
      define print_ch;

      const
                  max_buf = 127;
                  bufsize   = max_buf + 1;
      var
                  buf : array[0..max_buf] of char;
                  next_in, next_out              : 0..max_buf;
                  count                          : 0..bufsize;
                  data_ready, room_ready   : signal;


      procedure print_ch(c :char);
      begin
            if count = bufsize  then
                        wait(room_ready) end; {if}
            buf[next_in]        := c;
            next_in             := (next_in + 1) mod bufsize;
            count               := count + 1;
            send(data_ready)
      end print_ch;


      process print_driver[70B];  {interrupt vector address}
      const
            int_enable          = 6;
      var
            keyb_data_reg [177560B] : char;
            keyb_stat_reg [177562B] : bits;
      begin
            loop
                  if count = 0 then
                              wait(data_ready) end; {if}
                  keyb_data_reg    := buf[next_out];
                  next_out         := (next_out+1) mod bufsize;
                  count            := count - 1;
                  send(room_ready);
                  keyb_stat_reg[int_enable] := true;
                  doio;    {wait for interrupt}
                  keyb_stat_reg[int_enable] := false;
            end {loop}
      end print_driver;
```

begin
        next_in   := 0;
        next_out := 0;
        count   := 0;
        print_driver   {start interrupt routine}
end *printer;*

Fig. 7.7: Device interface module written in Modula.

The synchronous communication of CSP is more appropriate for the direct implementation of communication with devices. In his paper, Hoare (1978) suggests that input and output commands could be used to communicate with processes that are implemented in the hardware of peripheral devices. In fact, the architecture of the transputer and its programming language occam (May, 1985), are heavily based upon CSP. However, the implementation of CSP directly on traditional processor architectures would require the extension of its notation to specify the mapping of processes onto hardware devices and memory addresses. However, CSP does provide the basic concepts of synchronisation and data transfer needed to communicate with peripheral devices.

7.5. SUMMARY

This chapter has introduced some of the typical hardware features found in modern processors. In recent years, hardware architectures have evolved to incorporate and support useful concepts that have developed in software. This is seen in the hardware relative-addressing mechanisms and stacks to support block-structured program design, in the introduction of hardware procedure call and return mechanisms, and in support for multiple process contexts.

Interfacing to peripheral devices remains somewhat disorganised, but it is slowly becoming more coherent. The difficulty of interfacing to peripheral devices is due to two factors. The first factor is the inherent difficulty of designing and testing concurrent systems, a problem which can be overcome by the use of higher level conceptualisations and implementation techniques. The second source of difficulties lies in the poor design of device interfaces and in the inconsistent behaviour of different devices. With the falling costs of hardware, these problems are being tackled with better hardware designs and more hardware support in the device interface. The ever-decreasing costs of hardware means that device control logic is becoming extremely sophisticated and many devices now use on-board microprocessors as their controllers. This should result in simpler, more standardised interfaces and relieve the central processor from the detailed control and from the time-critical functions. Eventually, peripheral devices will provide a uniform, high-level interface to the processor and the problems of dealing with the peripheral hardware will be confined to the control logic embedded within them.

8

Programming Distributed Systems

8.1. INTRODUCTION

The previous chapters of this book have considered the programming of concurrent systems but have tended to either ignore the details of the underlying hardware or assume that the concurrency is provided by multiplexing a single processor between the software processes. This chapter will examine some of the complications that are encountered when software is developed for a distributed multiprocessor system.

The development of microprocessor-based single board computers and advances in communication technologies in the late 1970s initiated a rush of proposals for multicomputer and distributed systems. Unfortunately, these systems are still largely unrealised. The disparity in maturity between hardware and software engineering contributed to this situation. Hardware engineering is a relatively mature topic with a number of well defined standards and interfaces. Thus, multicomputers could be easily constructed from the available technology and it was assumed that any accommodation to a distributed environment could be made in the software. The simplicity of the hardware problems led people to underestimate the `difficulty of producing properly engineered software solutions.

The intense research activity of subsequent years has yielded a more mature understanding of the problems of a distributed environment for particular classes of applications. Distributed operating systems attempt to hide the distributed nature of the hardware from application programs and to provide a uniform interface to all the resources of the system. Distributed database systems attempt to provide increased performance and higher availability by distributing data, and sometimes by replicating it at a number of sites. Distributed computer control systems (DCCS) attempt to improve the response times and increase the sophistication of control systems by incorporating more processing power into remote equipment, leaving the central processor with a more supervisory and administrative role.

The insights derived from such systems can be generalised into programming methodologies which support a wide range of distributed applications. The aim of a 'distributed programming language' is to specify the operation of a 'distributed program', i.e. a single program which defines the operation of a distributed system. A distributed architecture has inherent problems which must be overcome by all software methodologies. However, it is usually assumed that despite the additional problems there will be an overall improvement in system performance in terms of cost, performance, reliability and flexibility.

The two example systems that have been used throughout this book could be implemented as distributed systems. The data-logger example would map simply onto a multiple processor architecture. The underlying hardware configuration is liable to constrain the input and output processes to be resident at the processors to which the peripheral devices are interfaced. However, the calculation process could co-reside with either process, could use a third processor or could be dynamically relocatable within the system. The optimum placement depends on the detailed balancing of the processing requirements against the reduction in communications overheads. These calculations must allow for any transformations of the format or encoding of information on heterogeneous systems. The complexities of partitioning such a simple system indicate the scale of problems that are encountered with multiple processes interacting in complex and varying patterns. The problems become further compounded if the system is designed to provide enhanced reliability by introducing redundant components and reconfiguring the system in case of any failure.

A probable implementation of the carpark controller example would be for each gate to have a dedicated processor on which the gate-controlling processes would be implemented. Again there are several ways in which the *space_control* module could be implemented: it could constantly reside at a single processor, be relocatable within the system, or be implemented in a distributed manner and reside at several sites.

This chapter will consider the topics relevant to the implementation of distributed programs. The significant difference between conventional and distributed programs is the need for inter-processor communication; the traditional approaches to the topic and their influence on the overall design of a system are introduced in the next section. The second section considers the problems of software development for distributed systems, such as the need to partition a program and configure it to suit the underlying hardware. The third section considers the ways in which traditional ways of structuring concurrent programs can be used in a distributed environment, and the final section examines the problems of maintaining the consistency of data in a distributed system.

8.2. COMMUNICATIONS ARCHITECTURES

The topic of communications networks is extensive and complex; a good introduction may be found in the book by Tanenbaum (1981). This section attempts only to introduce some of the central themes that have a significant influence on the services offered to the programmer and consequently influence the structuring of programs. This superficial presentation can be defended since the goal of most communication systems is to shield the user from as many implementation details as possible and to provide a simple, transparent service.

The term 'communication architecture' refers to the software support provided by the system as well as referring to the underlying hardware mechanisms for transmission of information between processes. The information to be transmitted is usually broken up by the communication system into standard sized objects and assembled with other information, such as its source and destination addresses and a checksum, to form a 'packet'. Packets are then transmitted over the communications system to the destination site; the transmission of packets may involve routing them through intermediary sites. At the destination site the packets are dismantled and the reconstituted data is delivered to the customer process.

Networks attempt to provide the user with a simple interface and attempt to implement all of the network-specific functions within the communications software. In general, communications software is developed as a number of layers of protocols. Each layer builds on the services provided by the subordinate layers and provides an enhanced service for the higher levels. As protocols are developed and standards become established, it is economic for the software to be transformed into special purpose hardware in the form of VLSI chips. A benefit of the multi-layer model is that these changes can occur at the lower levels without affecting the services provided to the upper levels.

The initial impetus for the development of computer communications systems came in the 1960s with the need to connect remote terminals and peripheral devices to mainframe processors. These systems were based on serial communications links which radiated out from the central processor in an irregular star shaped network, as illustrated in Fig. 8.1. Initially, the competing computer manufacturers developed proprietary protocols to govern the transmission of information within their networks. The protocols of the different manufacturers tended to be incompatible which prevented the networks from sharing information or equipment. The US government responded to this problem by funding the development of a national communications network to interconnect the computers of a number of their institutions which undertook advanced research projects. This was the ARPAnet

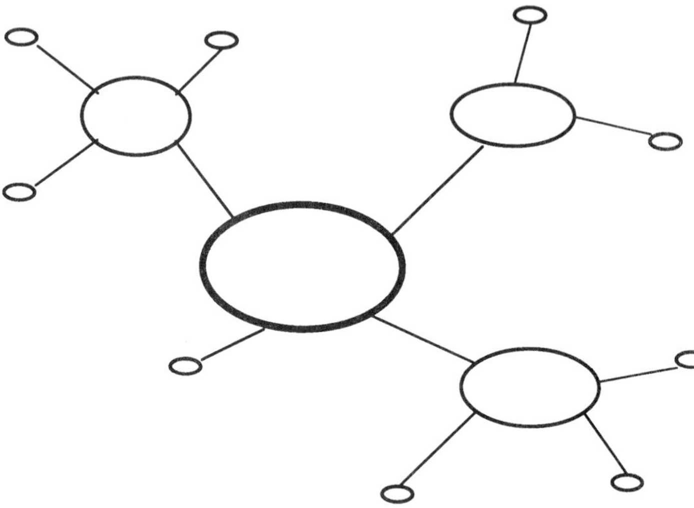

Fig. 8.1 - An irregular network.

project (McQuillian, 1977), subsequently renamed DARPAnet in recognition of the fact that most of the research is for US DoD purposes. Experience gained on ARPAnet influenced the development of the International Standards Organisation's 'Open Systems Interconnection' model (ISO OSI), which attempts to define general standards for the interconnection of computer systems.

8.2.1. The OSI reference model

The 'Open Systems Interconnection' model has been under development by the ISO since 1977. The reference model attempts to define a comprehensive set of protocols which will allow computers and other intelligent devices to communicate. Networks that are implemented using the model are 'open' since they do not use proprietary protocols and therefore will not be restricted to using equipment that is supplied by a particular manufacturer. Once the OSI model has been fully defined and implemented it is expected to dominate all inter-computer communications. It is therefore liable to have a profound effect on the way in which distributed programs will be structured. The approach taken in the OSI reference model is to identify a series of seven protocol layers. Each layer builds upon the services offered by the subordinate layers to offer an enhanced service for the upper layers, this policy is illustrated in Fig. 8.2. Application processes that need to communicate with each other but which reside on separate processors may call upon the services offered by the top layer of protocols. These are quite high-level services such as *send message* or *receive message*. Each layer of the protocol then processes the request and calls a series of lower-level operations that are provided by the subordinate layer. Eventually the bottom layer is reached and a series of messages are physically transmitted to another machine by the communications hardware. At the destination machine the messages are passed up the layers of protocols and reformed into the original message, which is delivered to the application process. The operations provided by the layers of the OSI model are as follows:-

(1) **Physical layer:** this provides the encoding, transmission and decoding of information to transfer uninterpreted strings of bits from one machine to another.

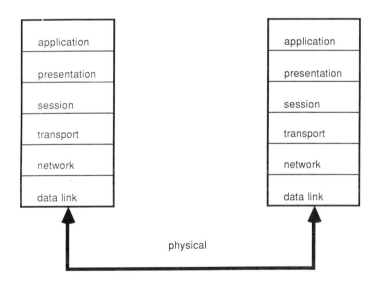

Fig. 8.2 - ISO OSI reference model.

(2)   **Data link:** this provides the protocols which control the flow of information over the link; it implements some error detection protocols and arranges for corrupted information to be retransmitted.

(3)   **Network layer:** the third layer implements higher level functions concerning the routing of messages from one machine to another and the forwarding of messages between intermediary sites.

(4)   **Transport layer:** the fourth layer implements a 'transport service' which moves information from one machine to another. The services that are offered by this layer are independent of the underlying mechanisms that are used by the lower three layers to transmit information. Information may travel over a number of communications channels using differing technologies, and the details should be hidden from the customers of the transport layer.

(5)   **Session layer:** this provides the protocols concerned with the establishment of dialogues between processes, such as establishing the connections and confirming the authenticity and authority of a customer process to request services.

(6)   **Presentation layer:** this layer implements the mapping between the representations of information used on different machines. The lower layers are concerned with the transmission of uninterpreted information between processes; the presentation layer is concerned with its meaning. The services provided by this layer range from the low-level mapping, such as from one character set to another, to the the representations of higher level objects, such as arrays, records or graphical representations of information.

(7)   **Application layer:** which provides the high level functions or utility services provided by the network, such as mail systems and protocols for accessing remote databases.

Unfortunately, progress in defining the details of the upper layers of the OSI model has been very slow, and much of the model has yet to be implemented. However, the model has been widely accepted and a good deal of effort is being put into its development. The model is also influencing the design of other communications systems which often adopt a similar partitioning and provide similar functions. Unfortunately, the development of the model has been dominated by communications specialists and it is oriented towards establishing one-to-one connections across a communications network. It is less suited to supporting the more complex patterns of interaction that are envisaged by programmers who work on distributed systems.

8.2.2. Transports services

The nature of the lower levels of the communications system have a strong influence on the services that can be provided by the upper layers, which, in turn, restricts the ways in which distributed programs can be implemented. This section will examine the relationships between these levels.

The structure of the lower three layers of a communications system are dependent on the nature of the underlying communications medium. Three configurations have dominated the developments in communications networks since the late 1970s. These are:-

(1) **Irregular networks:** which are based on serial communications links between machines, this topography has dominated wide area networks (WANs), such as DARPAnet.

(2) **Ring Networks:** in which each processor is connected to only two neighbours to form a ring. All messages are passed around the ring from source to destination. Rings tend to use high speed communications links and are therefore limited to geographically restricted areas, such as within one building. These smaller networks are referred to as 'local area networks' (LANs). Early development of ring networks was performed on the Cambridge Ring (Wilkes, 1980). Rings have gained commercial significance since the adoption of the Token Ring by IBM (IEEE, 1984).

(3) **Bus Systems:** in which all processors are connected to a common communications medium and data is broadcast to all sites. Within very restricted areas a parallel electronic bus may be used. Bus-based systems are usually restricted to LANs which use high frequency transmission over a single serial bus. These are referred to as CSMA (Carrier Sense Multiple Access), the most famous of such systems being Ethernet (Metcalf, 1976).

These low-level configurations may limit the range of facilities that are available at higher levels. In general, two forms of service are offered by the transport layer, level 4 of the OSI model. These are 'connectionless' and 'connection-oriented services', which are also referred to as 'datagram' and 'virtual circuit' services respectively, by analogy with traditional telegraph and telephone services.

Connectionless services, or datagrams, offer a lower standard of service. The network makes a 'best effort to deliver' messages, but it does not guarantee that messages will be delivered, nor that they will not be corrupted in transit, nor that they will be delivered in the order in which they were transmitted. The higher level protocols or the application processes must assume responsibility for checking the integrity of messages and for arranging for error recovery procedures if messages get lost or damaged in transit. Although LANs tend to be very reliable and error recovery is seldom used, it does need to be provided and this represents a significant programming overhead.

Connection-oriented, or virtual circuit, services build upon a datagram service to give a guaranteed service for the delivery of correctly sequenced, uncorrupted messages. All error detection and recovery is undertaken by the network protocols. Before messages can be transmitted, the connection must be established between the two customer processes; this requires that both parties to a communication inform the network software that they wish to establish a connection. This is done by calling the appropriate procedures that are provided by the network software. Once the connection is established, communication proceeds in the usual manner, but with the enhanced performance. On completion, the connection is closed using another procedure call, and connections to other processes can be established. Connectionless and connection-oriented services are not inherently incompatible and a network may offer the option of using either service, although obviously both parties to any exchange must use the same protocol.

In Chapter 4, four possible patterns of inter-process communication were identified: one-to-one, n-to-one, one-to-n and m-to-n. Table 8.1 summarises the ability of the different communications topographies and transport services to implement these patterns. Simple one-to-one dialogues, in which both parties are aware of the other's identity, can be established on all the network topographies using either connection-oriented or connectionless protocols. Connection-oriented protocols are ideally suited to this pattern of interaction. Connectionless protocols are less suited and some messages that arrive from processes other the current partner of the process may need to be buffered by the the application program.

N-to-one patterns, such as those found in programs structured on a client/server model, can also be supported on all the communications topographies. Connectionless transport services are ideally suited to this pattern. The short duration of the connection and the small quantity of data that is exchanged in each transaction means that connection-oriented protocols are less suitable because of the additional overhead of establishing the connection.

Communication	Topography			Transport Service	
Pattern	Bus	Ring	Irregular	Connection-oriented	Connectionless
1-to-1	yes	yes	yes	yes	possible
N-to-1	yes	yes	yes	no	yes
1-to-N	yes	yes	no	no	yes

Table 8.1 - Communications architectures and program structures.

One-to-N patterns, or broadcasts, are usually restricted to LANs, and are impractical to implement on irregular networks. Both bus and ring networks implement broadcasts by designating a special 'broadcast' or 'wildcard' address which is recognised at every site. On a bus system the broadcast reaches every site almost simultaneously. In a ring network the message is accepted at each site in turn as the message is passed around the ring. Broadcasts require a connectionless protocol, and a connection-oriented transport service is not suitable for implementing this pattern.

8.3. DISTRIBUTED PROGRAMMING SYSTEMS

The existence of multiple, disjoint processor address spaces within a distributed system introduces the need to partition the software components to suit the hardware configuration. To accommodate this partitioning, the logical structure of the software is usually defined as a collection of cooperating modules which are then mapped onto the target hardware. This mapping of the logical structures onto the physical hardware can be performed at one of three stages in the implementation of the system: early in the design phase; at a linkage phase after the logical modules have been implemented but before the program is executed; or during the program's execution. The first two options usually result in a static program structure, but the third option allows more dynamic program structures to be developed.

A distributed programming system, has to meet three basic requirements: the ability to define well encapsulated program modules with clearly identified communications paths between them; the ability to specify the logical to physical mapping of these components; and a method of disseminating the names of system components so that they can communicate. Some techniques that have been used to meet these requirements are discussed in the following sections.

8.3.1. Partitioning

The disjoint nature of process address spaces on a distributed system means that, in general, the use of physical addresses within inter-process communications is meaningless. The components of messages or parameters to remote procedure calls must consist of data values, and any returned information must be explicitly passed back. Optimisations such as passing only references to large data structures are not available unless both parties to a communication are known to reside on the same processor, in which case the inherent delays that are introduced by the need to transmit information physically can be avoided. Some design methods allow the designer to exploit this advantage by partitioning the software at an early stage in the overall system design and targeting it to a particular hardware configuration.

The Mascot system (Bate, 1986) is a well established example of such a design aid. It is oriented to the specification of large systems which are developed as a series of independent program modules which are then integrated to form a single concurrent system. Mascot defines a series of conventions concerning the representation of program modules and their inter-connections, using both a graphical and a textual notation. In graphical form, processes are represented by circles, shared data structures (such as monitors) are represented by rectangles, and their inter-relationships are represented by arrows. Mascot also allows the designer to specify the parameters of the interface between program modules. The program modules are developed in a sequential programming language, and are then integrated to form a single system using the Mascot specification. The third version of Mascot introduced conventions for the decomposition of program modules into collections of submodules. These conventions can be used to indicate the physical compo-sition of the system in the form of processors and communication links, which are then decomposed into program modules within each processor. A disadvantage of the Mascot approach is its failure to integrate the specification of the program structure with the code of its modules. This leads to undesirable complexity in the management of software development and maintenance.

The incorporation of configuration-specific information into a design at an early stage restricts its portability. This inhibits the use of cross-development techniques where software is produced and tested on hardware that differs from the target system. Early partitioning also means that upgrad-ing the target hardware is a more complicated operation. The problems can be avoided by developing configuration-independent software and then speci-fying the target hardware and allocation strategy at the linkage-editing phase.

The language *MOD (Starmod) (Cook, 1980; Leblanc, 1984) partly overcomes these problems by extending Modula with features which allow the underlying hardware configuration to be partially specified within a pro-gram, using **processor modules** and **network modules**. A processor module is used to encapsulate groups of processes and modules that should be imple-mented together on one physical processor. The compiler generates different code for the communication between processes depending on whether they are defined within the same or in separate processor modules; the former communications can exploit a shared address space, while in the latter case a call to the underlying communication system is generated. The network module defines the connectivity between the processor modules; the connec-tivity is expressed as a list of the pairs of processors which can communicate directly. For example, four processors connected in a unidirectional ring would be defined as:-

> **network module** *ring* =   *(node_1, node_2),*
>   *(node_2, node_3),*
>   *(node_3, node_4),*
>   *(node_4, node_1);*

Two processes can communicate directly only if their processor modules are linked in the network module definition.

The processor module and network module definitions of *MOD do not in fact define the hardware configuration and software allocation strategy; they merely constrain the possible target configurations. The mapping of processor modules into physical processors is specified at the link-loading phase, at which point a number of processor modules can be allocated to the same processor. When the program is loaded into the system, these mappings are conveyed to the underlying kernels which are responsible for the routing of all communications between processor modules; as a result the kernel may become involved in the communication between distinct software entities that have been mapped onto the same processor. The separation of the specification of the logical configuration from the specification of the physical configuration has the advantage that a change of physical configuration does not always necessitate a change or recompilation of the application program.

A similar approach is taken in SR (Andrews, 1982), which was introduced in Chapter 5. SR's **resources** encapsulate data, procedures and processes which must reside on a single processor. They communicate with other resources using remote operations. Like *MOD's processor modules, several resources can be mapped onto a single processor when the system is configured; however, this does not affect the structure of the resource in any way: it changes only the operations that are performed by the kernels to implement the remote operations.

8.3.2. Configuration

*MOD and SR both provide only static system configurations: all program modules are declared and allocated before the program is executed. However, it is sometimes useful for the configuration of a program to change or to evolve while the program is running, for example in communication or control applications where it is inconvenient or impossible to halt the entire system.

The Conic system (Kramer, 1983), developed at Imperial College, London, tackles this problem. The system comprises a programming language (Kramer, 1984) and a configuration language (Dulay, 1984). The programming language, which is based on Pascal, allows the definition of encapsulated task types which communicate solely by message exchange. Tasks declare a number of **ports** through which they communicate using **send** and **receive** operations. The data-type of a port must be declared, which allows the compiler to ensure the integrity of the language. However, the programming language does not allow the specification of the interconnection of ports; this facility is provided by the configuration language.

The Conic configuration language allows the configuration of a system to be specified in a configuration program. The program begins by importing context definitions that specify data types and task definitions from files which are produced by the programming language compiler. These definitions are then used in **create** statements to instantiate the tasks in the system, to supply their initial parameters, and to specify the processor to which they are allocated. The final part of the program then defines the inter-connection between input ports and output ports; the type compatibility of the ports can be checked using the definitions imported to the configuration program with the module definitions.

The configuration language allows the programmer to combine task definitions into structures similar to **records** or **arrays**, to help manage the construction of large systems. **Group modules** are analogous to record structures since they allow the definitions of new types of objects to be formed from a number of component processes whose ports are interconnected. These definitions can then be used within other **group modules** to give a hierarchically structured system.

Families of modules can be defined which give one-dimensional arrays from which the individual processes can be selected using an index. Definitions of families create associated families of entry-ports and exit-ports which are handled in a sensible manner.

The program specified in the configuration language is processed by a 'configuration manager' which validates the specification and issues low-level operating system commands to perform a series of operations. These operations cause the program code of the application tasks to be loaded; instances of tasks to be created and their parameters to be initialised; the communications channels to be initialised; and finally the execution the application program to be started. All these operations are also performed by the control software of all other distributed systems such as *MOD and SR. However, Conic also provides the facilities to define a change of configuration once the execution of the application program has started; new components may be added or substituted for existing elements, and the links between ports can be reconfigured. The changes to the configuration of a running system are defined in a configuration program which is then processed by the configuration manager to ensure that the resulting program would be a legitimate configuration. The configuration manager then issues further operating system commands to reconfigure the system; these may involve stopping and deleting tasks and unlinking connections as well as creating and linking new components.

Conic allows a system designer to specify the controlled reconfiguration of a software system from one stable state to another; once reconfigured, the system maintains a static configuration until further modification is required. The particular advantage of the Conic approach is the flexibility it offers by separating the definition of the components of a system from the creation and configuration of the system.

This approach contrasts with that of dynamic programming languages. Programs in these languages change their configuration during their execution by creating new processes, for example, by using the **fork** procedure in Mesa to create a new process. Although the configuration of the executing system can change over time, the potential range of configurations is established within the program and cannot be amended or extended once execution has begun.

Choosing the optimum site for the execution of a process can be difficult if it interacts with a number of other modules, or if the patterns of process interaction may vary over time, so some systems attempt dynamic reconfiguration and relocate software modules during program execution to reflect their usage or to compensate for hardware failures. For example, Casey (1977) examined the possibilities for the operating system to relocate processes automatically within a distributed system depending on the resources they required and on the dynamic work load of the system. However, the development of these techniques has been very slow because of the complex interrelationship between local load scheduling and resource allocation policies and the global performance of the system.

8.3.3. Naming

The flexibility of the options for the configuration of a program are restricted by the services that are offered by the underlying support software which controls the naming of objects, the dissemination of the names, and the routing of messages to their destinations.

A single, statically configured program on a single processor can use the address of an object within the processor's memory to name the object. The dissemination of the names and the routing of messages is performed by the compiler and the linkage-editor. When the objects are more dynamic the operating system must provide these services, for example by managing filenames which are used to link processes to data objects and by handling process identifiers which are used to route messages to processes. The operating system controls the allocation of names, ensures that they are always unique, and keeps tables of information which relate the names of objects to their physical addresses.

A distributed environment introduces two problems: simple physical addresses are no longer unique, and it is usually impractical to keep a single table that relates names to addresses. Several techniques have been adopted to tackle these problems.

The most simple strategy to overcome the first of these problems is to give each processor a unique name which is incorporated into the name of all objects that reside at the processor. Provided that objects are not relocated to other processors, the underlying communications protocols are able to determine the destination of a message directly from the name of the recipient.

If objects are to be relocated, another scheme for generating names must be adopted; otherwise, if a series of objects were generated at the same memory location and then relocated, they would all be given the same name. One solution to this problem is to include the time of generation, as well as the place, into the name of an object. Sometimes a random component is also included into the name; this enhances the security of the system since it greatly reduces the chances that a process can generate a valid name by either erroneously or maliciously corrupting a legitimate one.

The use of location-independent names means that routing messages to their destinations is more difficult. The communications software needs to be able to determine the location of every named object, rather than simply needing to know the fixed locations of the processors. The Distributed Computer System (DCS), (Farber, 1972), is an early example of a system that tackled the problem of location-independent names and allowed the possibility of the migration of software modules. It was a loop system which had additional hardware interface units between the loop and each processor. Each 'interface unit' contained an associative memory which contained the names of the processes resident at the processor that it served. This combined fast message handling with location-independent names, and allowed processes to migrate to another processor without informing the processes with which they communicated. The same strategy can also be applied on a bus architecture, since the destinations of all messages are examined at every site.

Within a large irregular network the problems of mapping logical names to physical addresses, and routing messages to their correct destination is more complex. The Grapevine system (Birrell, 1982, Schroeder, 1984) developed by Xerox is an interesting distributed solution to the problem. Grapevine implements a message passing system between sites in a network and also maintains a distributed, replicated, database. The two aspects of Grapevine call on each other's services: the database uses the message system to distribute the update messages to keep replicated copies of information consistent, and the message system uses the database to maintain information about the destinations for messages. The main purpose of Grapevine is to provide a distributed, resilient, electronic mail system for users, but it has also been used to provide the name-resolution and communication facilities for distributed programs. Modules within a distributed program which provide services, such as a file server module, publish details of their name, address and the services that they offer in the distributed database. Client modules then use Grapevine to retrieve this information and obtain the name of a suitable server module; they then use Grapevine's message facility to access these services. Using Grapevine in this manner introduces two problems that will be encountered in any general-purpose distributed system. One problem is the coordination of the updating of the multiple copies of a database item when it is changed or deleted, this topic is considered in section 8.5. The other problem is the slow response of the communications system, which is a common failing of general-purpose systems when their performance is compared to the potential performance of an optimised system designed for a more specific purpose, such as the systems discussed in section 8.4.2.

8.4. CONCURRENT PROGRAMS ON DISTRIBUTED SYSTEMS

This section will examine the way in which conventional concurrent programs, such as those that have been examined in this book, can be implemented in a distributed environment. Concurrent languages are usually structured to provide independent modules with clear communications paths; these modules are usually distributed among the available processors and the inter-process communications are provided by some message-based communications software of the form outlined earlier in section 8.2.

8.4.1. Message based languages

There is a close fit between the services offered by most communications systems and the requirements of an asynchronous message-based programming language. Given the successful delivery of a message to a process, the distributed nature of the hardware architecture does not impose any additional constraints on message acceptance in an asynchronous message facility. However, it is more difficult to implement in a synchronous message methodology because of the extensive communications protocols and the resulting propagation delays that arise from the use of any form of communications network. The close synchronisation of processes required in CSP, and related languages such as occam (Inmos, 1984), is oriented towards the more direct connections found in specialised hardware such as multiprocessors or networks of transputers (May, 1985) rather than in general networks. The implementation of communication commands in the guard of a guarded command can be difficult since it requires the negotiated agreement of both parties as to when to proceed. This means that a simple message exchange at the program level leads to a multi-message dialogue at the time of execution. The problem is exacerbated if both input and output commands may appear in guards, since neither party to a communication will commit itself to waiting indefinitely for the other, and very complex protocols are required even for non-distributed systems (Buckley, 1983).

As noted previously, the logger maps very simply onto an asynchronous message methodology, which in turn maps simply onto a small multiple processor architecture. An asynchronous message implementation automatically provides any buffering or demon processes needed to move messages around, so that the implementation of the logger is trivially simple.

Using a synchronous message methodology necessitates the introduction of buffer processes. These buffers could be allocated their own processors but it is probably better for them to reside on the same processor as their producer process, in effect this would implement an asynchronous message facility.

One of the motivations for the message methodology was to relieve the applications programmer of all problems concerning the sharing or the coordination of access to data. Implementing the carpark controller within the spirit of this methodology would require that the *space_control* functions of tracking the resource usage and of queuing requests should be performed by a single process. This process may require a dedicated processor because of its relatively high intensity of communications-related processing; alternatively, it may share a particular gate-controlling processor or migrate between processors. The brief nature of the messages and the fact that there may be a significant delay between the request for a space and its allocation means that a connectionless communications protocol is more appropriate for this system, rather than incurring the additional overheads of establishing a connection for each transaction.

8.4.2. Implementing distributed monitors

Although distributed systems lack memory that is directly shared, there are three techniques which allow programs that are based on the monitor concept to be implemented:-

Centralised Monitors:
> A single copy of the monitor always resides at one site and is accessed by remote procedure calls. The implementation of a monitor system in this manner is similar to the implementation of operation oriented systems which are considered in the next section.

Migrating Monitors:
> A single copy of the monitor migrates around the sites and is accessed by the local processes.

Distributed Monitors:
> Several copies of a monitor exist which are resynchronised or resolved occasionally. This approach is dependent on the possibility of partitioning the monitor variables and on developing stringent controls over the behaviour of the variables within each partition such that overall consistency is always maintained.

Each of these three methods are dependent upon some underlying message facility to provide the transportation either of procedure parameters and results, monitor data or synchronisation and update messages respectively. All techniques may be used on any network topography, but the latter two methods are most efficiently implemented on those which support a broadcast mechanism.

Both the data-logger and the carpark controller may be implemented using each of these mechanisms. The first alternative, that of using remote procedure calls to access a monitor, is covered in more detail in the next section. For the data-logger, two monitors are used to implement inter-process buffers between the three processes. Each buffer should be located locally to its associated producer process, since it is quicker to access a local procedure than a remote one and the input process has the most severe timing constraints. For the carpark controller, the *space_control* monitor can be located anywhere in the system provided that it can be accessed by all the processors.

When implementing the data-logger using 'migrating' monitors, it may be viable for the calculation and output processes (*calculator* and *outputter*) of the data-logger to reside on different processors and for the data to be moved in the *buffer* by the underlying monitor access mechanisms. When a process attempts to access a monitor, its execution is delayed until the monitor is resident at the same site as the process and is not being accessed by another process; this is a logical generalisation of the gate mechanisms which delay the execution of monitor procedures in order to enforce mutual exclusion of access. Verjus (1983) proposed that the monitor should visit each site in sequence, moving to the next when there are no outstanding requests for access at its current site. Other researchers (Casey, 1977; Whiddett, 1983) have suggested that the underlying support software should queue requests for access to each monitor, which then migrates between sites on demand.

Whichever mechanism is used to implement monitor migration, moving monitors between sites is bound to be a time-consuming operation which may not meet the timing constraints of the input process of the data-logger. The *inputter* and *calculator* processes may therefore be constrained to reside at the same processor so that the buffer monitor need not move.

An alternative implementation technique would be to have a pool of buffer monitors that circulate between the two processes, thus providing another level of buffering. The *inputter* would fill each buffer in sequence,

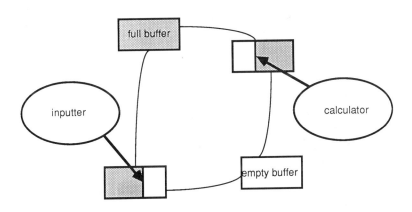

Fig. 8.3 - A pool of migrating monitors.

during which time the buffer could remain at the same site. Once full, the buffer could migrate to the *calculator's* processor to be emptied while the *inputter* fills another buffer; this structure is illustrated in Fig. 8.3. This technique would allow the processes to reside on separate processors; unfortunately, it adds an extra level of complexity to the software.

For the carpark, the gate controlling processes would remain located at each processor, and *space_control* would migrate between the sites and would be updated with the number of cars that had entered or departed through the gate since *space_control's* previous visit to that gate. When the carpark is nearly full to capacity, the policy of having the monitor visit each site in sequence may lead to unfair scheduling, because spaces vacated by cars leaving one exit will be allocated to customers waiting at the next entrance even if there are customers at other entrances who have been waiting longer. The methods of queuing access requests overcome this problem and implement a fairer policy, but they require more support from the underlying software.

The final implementation technique involves maintaining a copy of the monitor at each site, and imposing more rigid constraints on their access than are necessary when there is a single copy. For the data-logger example, the buffer area of the monitor can be partitioned between the producer and consumer processes according to whether or not it is in use. The producer is allowed to access only the unused portion of the buffer and update the index variable, *next_in*, within these bounds (see Fig. 8.4). Similarly the consumer process is granted access to only the portion of the buffer that is known to be occupied. Periodically some underlying mechanism is invoked to resynchronise the copies of the monitor. At this time the new input data is passed to the copy of the monitor residing with the consumer process, and the constraints on the index variables are adjusted to reflect the current usage of the buffer.

With the carpark example, the *space_control* monitor is replicated at each of the processors, but each incarnation of the monitor is constrained to allocated only its share of the available spaces before the monitor is resynchronised. During the resynchronisation operation the net effect of the actions of each incarnation of *space_control* is known and new quotas are established. The drawback of this approach is the complexity of the resynchronisation protocol and the difficulty of finding general methods of partitioning the variables. Similar techniques are employed in distributed databases, and Kohler (1981) provides a review of the techniques in this context. However, although databases encounter the same problems, they have the advantage of working on much longer time-scales than real-time systems.

8.4.3. Implementing remote operations

An advantage of operation-oriented systems is that the semantics of calling a remote operation may be very similar to those of calling a procedure; this simplifies the transition to a distributed environment for non-specialist programmers. The significant difference between a local procedure call and a remote operation is that the execution of the operation is performed in the

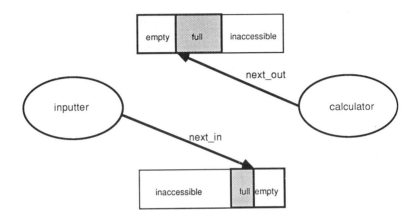

Fig. 8.4 - A partitioned monitor.

environment of the remote process. In Ada all the remote operations which are implemented by a server task are executed sequentially in the environment of the server. In DP the operations are performed by one of the set of anonymous process which are provided by each **process** to service requests to its operations. The caller sends the request and awaits the reply; the implementation determines whether the operation is local to the processor or if the request requires transmission over the communications network before it can be executed.

The implementation of remote operations can be based upon either a connection oriented (virtual circuit) or a connectionless (datagram) transport service. A connection-oriented service is very reliable, but it is very expensive to set up the connection considering the small amounts of data that are involved, which usually consist of only a few parameters and results. RPC mechanisms have been built upon standard connectionless protocols, but error control mechanisms need to be integrated into the calling mechanisms to compensate for the poorer quality of the transport service. Reliable operations are usually implemented by allocating a unique name to each invocation of a remote operation or transaction; the client process periodically sends repeat requests using the same name until an acknowledgement is received. The server process keeps track of the names of the transactions that it executes, and ignores any duplicate requests.

Even connectionless protocols involve a substantial overhead, and RPC mechanisms are now recognised as a special mode of communication that is significantly different from the usual 'byte-stream' communications. The performance of a system can be substantially improved by incorporating RPC mechanisms directly into the transport services offered by the communications system, (e.g. Birrell, 1984; Spector, 1982). The improvement in performance is often obtained by abandoning the traditional layered approach to the implementation of communications software and by providing a single layer of software between the application program and the hardware. This makes the communications software more complex to implement, but it greatly reduces the overheads of parameter passing and context swapping. The integration of remote operations can sometimes be taken further at the remote site where the communications software can directly implement the remote operation and initiate the response to the calling process, rather than passing the request to the local application program. The use of these integrated RPC transport services can reduce the communications delays by two orders of magnitude. However, even using high-speed links, such as ethernet, the communication delays are a significant overhead, and brief remote operations remain two orders of magnitude slower to execute when they are performed on separate machines rather than when they are implemented on the same processor.

8.5. CONSISTENCY IN DISTRIBUTED SYSTEMS

A major requirement of any concurrent programming system is that it should have the ability to ensure that all of the program modules have a consistent view of the overall state of the program and of the values of any shared variables. Implementations of concurrent systems on a single processor usually enforce this consistency by encapsulating groups of related items, and by restricting access to them so that they are always in a coherent state when a process gains or relinquishes its exclusive access to them. Unfortunately, these restrictive policies are incompatible with the goals of distributed systems which aim to provide higher availability and faster access to data. The long and unpredictable communications delays, and the higher probability of failure of some part of the system, usually lead to the replication of data at a number of sites within a distributed system. This section will introduce some of the techniques that can be used to tackle the problems of maintaining consistency of multiple copies of data items and of overcoming failures in distributed systems. The techniques were initially developed for database applications and are covered in more detail in Date's (1983) book. The integration of the techniques into some experimental distributed operating systems is described in some chapters in the book edited by Chambers (1984).

The failure of the central processor in a single processor system is usually catastrophic, and it allows no possibility of continued operation. Recovery is usually implemented by periodically recording the status of the entire system on some non-volatile memory, a process called 'checkpointing'.

Between checkpoints, the system logs the details of any transactions that modify the its state. If the system fails, the previously checkpointed state is restored, or 'rolled back', and the logged transactions are re-run to restore the system to the state it was in just before its failure.

This technique is more difficult to apply in a distributed system because of the difficulty of checkpointing the entire system simultaneously. In the event of an error, sites may have to be rolled back through several checkpoints before a consistent state is found for the entire system. This 'domino effect' arises if the checkpointing of sites does not coincide with their interactions. For example, site A might roll back to a point just before sends a message to site B, but site B might roll back to the point just after it has received the message. The restored state would be inconsistent, since B would have received a message that A would not consider that it had sent. The two sites could not be 'rolled forward' together, since A would retransmit the message, but B would have no record of receiving it.

A number of techniques for structuring distributed programs have been proposed which maintain consistency and aid recovery in distributed systems. Most schemes are dependent on each site having some 'stable storage'; redundant, non-volatile storage which allows information to survive a system failure (Needham, 1983). The information that is recorded on stable storage is updated by 'atomic transactions' which transform it from one consistent state to another. These mechanisms combine to keep the system in a consistent state and to minimise the need to roll back and to re-run the system.

8.5.1. Implementing stable storage

Disk files on conventional operating systems usually contain two forms of information: the data that is being stored for the application and indexing information that defines the structure of the file which is maintained by the operating system. To update the contents of a file, the data block containing the desired record must be read into the primary memory; its contents can then be changed, and the block must then be rewritten to the backing store. If the structure of the file is changed, for example if a record is expanded so that it occupies additional blocks, a number of index blocks will also need to be updated. The cycle of updating a file is obviously not indivisible or 'atomic', and the system could fail at any time which would leave the filing system in an inconsistent state. In fact, the writing of an individual block is not atomic, and the system can fail part of the way through writing a block, and leave it in a corrupted state.

The problems of a system crashing while it is writing an individual block may be overcome by duplicating every block of information. The duplicate block is only updated after the primary block has been successfully modified, so that the system always has at least one good copy of the data which may be used for error recovery.

The atomic updating of the file as a whole can be achieved by not updating the individual records, but by creating a new 'shadow file' in the updated form. All of the changes are then incorporated into the file at once by updating the master index block of the file; this is illustrated in Fig. 8.5. In this way the file is transformed from one consistent state to another in a single operation. If the index information is kept on stable storage, then one or other of the states may be restored from the duplicate block in the case of the system crashing during the update. These mechanisms combine to provide the secure storage of information at a single site, which is always in a coherent, recoverable state, and which may be updated in an atomic operation. The problem that remains is to synchronise the update of data that is either replicated or dispersed in a distributed system.

8.5.2. Synchronising replicated data

The 'multiple copy update problem' is usually solved in a centralised manner using a 'two phase commit' protocol (Grey, 1979). One site is designated as the 'update coordinator' for a particular transaction, responsible for ensuring that either all of the copies of the data are updated or none of them are changed within a 'cohort' of affected sites. At the start of the transaction the coordinator requests that each site prepares to execute the transaction and to reach a state where it may either commit the changes in an atomic operation, or abort the transaction completely.

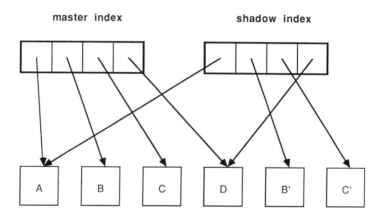

Fig. 8.5. - A shadow file.

Each site performs the requested operations and replies to the coordinator when it is in a position to commit the changes, or when it finds that it is incapable of executing the operation: for example, a distributed banking transaction might be aborted because the client's account is overdrawn. If any of the cohort cannot be contacted, or if any of them cannot agree to commit the changes, then the coordinator aborts the transaction and directs the members of the cohort to abort their individual sub-actions so that the system remains unchanged.

If all the cohort can agree to the change, the coordinator records its 'intention to commit' the transaction on stable storage. It then requests each site to commit the local sub-action and to confirm that they have done so. Once the decision to commit a transaction has been taken, the action cannot be aborted, and the coordinator is responsible for ensuring that every site commits the transaction. If any of the cohort crash before they have acknowledged that they have committed the changes, the coordinator must establish contact with them as soon as they are restarted and must ensure that the action is committed. These concepts are well established and have been incorporated into the framework of the programming language Argus (Liskov, 1983).

The requirement of unanimous agreement in the two-phase commit protocol can limit its operation in the event of a partial system failure which renders some sites inaccessible, or when some files may be stored off-line on removable backing store. Some systems that use replicated files employ a weakened version of the two-phase commit protocol, and require only that the majority of the copies of each file are updated for each transaction (Thomas, 1979). This method requires that each file must contain an indication of the time when it was last updated. The distributed filing system must ensure that application processes operate on the latest version of a file, and must automatically update the filestore of a processor when it is restarted after a failure.

8.6. SUMMARY

The aim of this chapter has been to introduce the major practical themes which have developed in programming distributed systems. Attempting to cover so large an area has necessitated some simplification and the omission of detail. The important topics of timing constraints, scheduling and preformance evaluation, among others, have been ignored in this discussion.

The implementation of dynamic general purpose distributed programs is a poorly developed subject. A better understanding of the general techniques has been gained from the study of distributed implementations of specific applications areas. However, further work on alternative techniques needs to be carried out. Although distributed systems have been discussed for many years, practical systems tend to be of limited size and fixed configuration. The full benefits of distributed systems will only be realised once the automation of scheduling, partitioning and failure control is achieved. Progress in the field of distributed systems would benefit from a greater emphasis on these aspects and on their support by the hardware. These aspects have tended to be neglected in comparison to the attention paid to the lower level communications aspects.

Traditionally, communications architectures provide fairly static configurations, and research has tended to concentrate on improving reliability and bandwidth. This static model is quite suitable for implementing asynchronous message facilities and simple communications-level RPC mechanisms. However, it is not suited either to synchronous message systems (the direction taken by the CSP family of languages), or to the conditional communication implicit in guarded commands and the rendezvous mechanism used in Ada. Implementing distributed programs is a very large problem and researchers tend to work either from the top down (i.e. through language development) or from the bottom up (from communications protocols). Unfortunately they seem to have been targeted on different goals since the late 1970s and some common aims need to be established to link the threads of these concurrent lines of research.

Appendix A

Programming with Data Structures

A.1. STACKS

The following Pascal program illustrates the programming of a stack which is implemented as an array of characters. The stack pointer, *sp*, points to the current top of the stack, so it indicates one less than the bottom of the stack when the stack is empty. The procedures *push*, and *pop* implement the stack operations; procedure *show* displays the contents of the stack. The main body of the program provides a simple interactive interface, and the program terminates when the end-of-file is indicated.

```
program stack (input, output);
const
        maxstack        = 12;
        minstack= 1;
        minsp           = 0;
type
        stackrange      = minstack..maxstack;
        sprange         = minsp..maxstack;
var
        sp      : sprange;
        stack   : array[stackrange] of char;
        tempch  : char;
        commands        : set of char;
```

```
procedure push (inc : char);
begin
        if sp < maxstack then
                begin
                        sp                      := sp + 1;
                        stack[sp]               := inc
                end
end;


procedure pop (var out : char);
begin
        if sp > minsp then
                begin
                        out     := stack[sp];
                        sp      := sp - 1
                end
        else
                out := '!'
end;


procedure show;
var
        i : integer;
begin
        writeln( 'top' );
        for i := sp downto minstack do
                writeln ( stack[i] );
        writeln( 'bottom' );
        writeln
end;


procedure help;
begin
        writeln(' The following commands are recognised:-');
        writeln('<  pop item from stack');
        writeln('>X  push character X onto stack');
        writeln(' =  display stack');
        writeln('?  display this message');
        writeln;
end;
```

```
begin
        commands := ['<','>','=','?'];
        sp := minsp;
        help;
        repeat
                while not eof and not( input↑ in commands) do
                        get(input);
                if not eof then
                        case input↑ of
                                '<':
                                        begin
                                                readln;
                                                pop(tempch);
                                                writeln(tempch)
                                        end;
                                '>':
                                        begin
                                                get(input);
                                                tempch := input↑;
                                                push(tempch);
                                                readln
                                        end;
                                '=':
                                        begin
                                                readln;
                                                show;
                                        end;
                                '?':
                                        begin
                                                readln;
                                                help;
                                        end
                        end;{case}
        until eof
end.
```

A.2. LINKED LISTS

The following program demonstrates the use of linked lists of records. Each element in the list consists of two components, a data item and a link to the next item, *next*. The end of the list is indicated by setting the value of the link to *nil*. The list starts with the variable *head*, which is given an initial value of *nil*.

To add an item to the list, first a new element is created and its fields are initialised to the value of the data, and the value *nil* to indicate that it is the end of the list. If the list is currently empty the head of the list is set to point to the new item; otherwise, the current end of the list is located by inspecting each element in turn until the last one is encountered. The new item is then appended to the list by modifying the link in the tail of the list.

To extract the first element from the list, the value of *head* is examined. If the list is empty its value is *nil* and an error is reported. Otherwise, the value of *head* is modified to indicate the remainder of the list, the value of the first element is extracted, and the list element is destroyed.

The procedure *show* works its way through the list displaying the contents of each element in turn until the end of the list is detected. The rest of the program provides the interface to the user and is very similar to that in the previous example.

```
program list(input, output);

type
        pelement        = ↑element;
        element         = record
                                data : char;
                                next : pelement
                        end;
var
        commands        : set of char;
        tempch          : char;
        head            : pelement;

procedure puttail (inch : char);
var
        newitem, temp : pelement;

begin
        new(newitem);
        newitem↑.data := inch;
        newitem↑.next := nil;
        if head = nil then
                head := newitem
        else
```

```
                          begin
                                  temp := head;
                                  while temp↑.next <> nil do
                                          temp := temp↑.next;
                                  temp↑.next := newitem
                          end
          end;


procedure gethead (var out : char);
var
          temp : pelement;

begin
          if head <> nil then
                          begin
                                  out  := head↑.data;
                                  temp := head;
                                  head := head↑.next;
                                  dispose(temp);
                          end
                  else
                          out := '!'
          end;


procedure show;
var
          temp : pelement;
begin
          writeln( 'head' );
          temp := head;
          while temp <> nil do
                          begin
                                  writeln (temp↑.data);
                                  temp := temp↑.next
                          end;
          writeln( 'tail' );
          writeln
          end;
```

```
procedure help;
begin
        writeln(' The following commands are recognised:-');
        writeln('<  pop item from stack');
        writeln('>X  push character X onto stack');
        writeln(' =  display stack');
        writeln('?  display this message');
        writeln;
end;


begin
        commands := ['<','>','=','?'];
        head := nil;
        help;
        repeat
                while not eof and not( input↑ in commands) do
                        get(input);
                if not eof then
                        case input↑ of
                                '<':
                                        begin
                                                readln;
                                                gethead(tempch);
                                                writeln(tempch)
                                        end;
                                '>':
                                        begin
                                                get(input);
                                                tempch := input↑;
                                                puttail(tempch);
                                                readln
                                        end;
                                '=':
                                        begin
                                                readln;
                                                show;
                                        end;
                                '?':
                                        begin
                                                readln;
                                                help;
                                        end
                        end;{case}
        until eof
end.
```

Appendix B

Solutions to Traditional Problems

No book on concurrent programming would be complete without a discussion of two of the traditional examples of concurrent systems: the readers and writers problem, and the dining philosophers' problem.

B.1. READERS AND WRITERS

The readers and writers problem is a model of a database system. It attempts to provide greater concurrency than a mutual exclusion protocol by allowing any number of processes to read a shared resource or a shared file concurrently. However, exclusive access is required for a write, or update, operation.

Most concurrent programming languages cannot express a complete solution to the problem, since the concept of mutual exclusion is often integrated into the language constructs. However, these languages can enforce the sequencing constraints and assume that the programmer can find a way to access the file directly. Ada allows a more complete solution to the problem since it is possible for tasks to share variables in an unrestricted manner. The discipline of the problem may then be imposed by the programmer by the introduction of a 'gatekeeping' task which synchronises the operation of the other tasks. The specification of the *gatekeeper* task is:-

```
task gatekeeper is
        entry start_read;
        entry end_read;
        entry start_write;
        entry end_write;
end gatekeeper;
```

A *reader* task is expected to call the *start_read* rendezvous to obtain permission to access the shared resource; once the rendezvous has been accepted the *reader* can then access the resource concurrently with other *readers*; when it has completed its access it informs the *gatekeeper* by calling the *end_read* rendezvous. A similar protocol must be followed by the *writers* using the other two entries; however, the *writers* must not proceed concurrently with each other or with the *readers*.

The body of the *gatekeeper* task is:-

```
task body gatekeeper is
        num_readers       : integer := 0;
        writing           : boolean := false;
begin
        loop
                select
                        when not writing =>
                                accept start_read;
                                num_readers := num_readers + 1;
                or
                        accept end_read;  --always let them finish
                        num_readers := num_readers - 1;
                or
                        when not writing and num_readers = 0 =>
                                accept start_write;
                                writing := true;
                or
                        accept end_write;
                        writing := false;
                end select;
        end loop;
end gate_keeper;
```

The relative priorities of *readers* and *writers* can be adjusted using more conditions in the guards. Note that the above solution gives priority to the *readers*, who can conspire to 'starve' the *writers*.

B.2. DINING PHILOSOPHERS

The 'dining philosophers' problem is a model of resource allocation in an operating system. Five philosophers live together in a house and spend most of their time thinking. At random intervals they become hungry and go to the dining room and sit at their usual place at the round table where their maid always keeps a large bowl of spagetti. The philosophers' general level of hygiene is rather lacking, and they possess only five forks between them, which they always leave on the table, one between each pair of places. When a philosopher wants to eat he picks up the two forks that are next to his place at the table. However, if one or other of his neighbours is already eating he may have to wait until that person has finished with the shared fork. The philosophers are rather apprehensive about this arrangement since a similar school of philosophy died out completely when they all turned up to eat simultaneously one night. They were discovered some months later, each starved to death with a fork clasped firmly in his left hand, a very gruesome and tragic affair. To avoid a similar fate, the philosophers agreed on the following protocol, a) only four philosophers are allowed into the dining room at any time; and b) they always pick the left fork up before the right fork, which prevents a pair of philosophers accidentally starving their colleague who sits between them.

The situation can be modelled in Concurrent Pascal:-

```
program philosophers;

type philosopher = process(dining_room: room; left, right: fork);
begin
        cycle
                <think>;
                dining_room.enter;
                left.pick_up;
                right.pick_up;
                <eat>;
                left.put_down;
                right.put_down;
                dining_room.leave
        end
end;

type fork = monitor;
var
        taken    : boolean;
        free     : queue;

        procedure entry pick_up;
        begin
                if taken then
                        delay( free );
                taken := true
        end;
```

```
              procedure entry put_down;
              begin
                      taken := false;
                      continue( free )
              end;

begin
        taken := false
end; {fork}

type room = monitor;
var
              diners   : integer;
              leaver   : queue;

              procedure entry enter;
              begin
                      if diners = 4 then
                              delay( leaver );
                      diners := diners + 1
              end;

              procedure entry leave;
              begin
                      diners := diners -1;
                      continue( leaver )
              end;

begin
        diners := 0
end; {room}

var     {main program}
        philosophers      : array[0..4] of philosopher;
        forks             : array[0..4] of fork;
        dining_room       : room;
        i                 : integer;

begin
        init dining_room;
        for i := 0 to 4 do
                init forks[i];
        for i := 0 to 4 do
                init philosophers[i]( dining_room, forks[i], forks[(i+1) mod 5]
end. {program}
```

Glossary

ASCII
: standard coding for computer character sets.

Actual parameter
: the values given to an instance of a formal parameter.

Address space
: range of memory locations accessible to a process.

Array
: data variable containing several components of the same type.

Atomic transaction
: high-level operation that is performed indivisibly.

Broadcast
: a message that may be received by all devices on the system.

Bus
: hardware device used to interconnect several devices.

Busy-waiting
: see Polling.

CE
: Concurrent Euclid, a concurrent programming language based on Euclid.

CP
: Concurrent Pascal, a concurrent programming language based on

Pascal.

CSMA

carrier sense multiple access, mechanism for accessing a broadcast communications medium.

CSP

Communicating Sequential Processes, a programming notation for concurrent systems.

Check digit

redundant information added to a message to allow the receiver to check for errors.

Coercion

mechanisms for changing the type of a variable.

Connection oriented

communications protocols which establish a guaranteed sequenced communication channel between two parties.

Connectionless

communications protocols which do not guarantee the sequenced delivery of messages.

DCCS

distributed computer control system, for large scale factory automation.

DMA

direct memory access, mechanism which connects peripheral devices to the memory.

DP

Distributed Processes, a programming language based on RPCs.

Datagram

see connectionless.

Deadlock

situation when a number of processes become delayed mutually waiting for each other to perform some operation.

Disjoint processes

processes that do not communicate or share data.

Distributed program

program that defines the concurrent operation of a number of interconnected processors.

EBCDIC

IBM's character coding scheme.

Formal parameter

the definition of the type of a parameter.

Function

a procedure whose execution returns a value to the calling program.

Guarded command
>   programming language construct used to indicate indeterminate operations.

Indivisible operation
>   operation that may not be interrupted, usually at a low level in the system.

Interrupt
>   hardware signal from a device to a processor to indicate the completion of an operation.

Invariant
>   expression that defines the desired constraints on a collection of data variables.

Kernel
>   fundamental collection of procedures to control the hardware.

MMU
>   memory management unit, hardware device restricting the processor's access to memory.

Memory mapping
>   method of connecting peripheral devices to the processor so that they may be addressed as memory locations.

Monitor
>   language construct that defines a program module for which mutual exclusion is enforced.

Multiprogramming
>   having several programs active simultaneously within a computer system.

Mutual exclusion
>   the policy for enforcing the correctness of programs by restricting access to data to one process at a time.

Online
>   interactive computer system without real-time constraints.

Operating system
>   collection of basic programs that control the operation of the hardware.

PSR
>   processor status register.

Packet
>   small message containing source and destination addresses that is transported by a communications system.

Parameter
>   mechanism to allow information to be passed between components of a program.

PLITS
    a programming language based on asynchronous message exchange.

Polling
    continual testing and re-testing of a data variable waiting for some condition.

Port addressing
    method of connecting peripheral devices to the processor .

Primitive data types
    data types for which operations are provided by the processor hardware.

Procedure
    a self-contained sequence of instructions within a program.

Process
    independent asynchronous activity within a processor.

Processor
    hardware device which executes the instructions of a program.

Program
    sequence of instructions .

Queue
    mechanism to allow the suspension of operation of a process.

RPC
    remote procedure call, used for process coordination.

Real-time
    a computer system that must respond within the timescale of the external environment.

Record
    data variable containing several components of differing types.

Reentrant procedure
    a procedure that may be executed concurrently by several processes.

Rendezvous
    synchronised process communication mechanism used in Ada.

SR
    Synchronised Resources, a concurrent programming language.

Select statement
    a form of guarded command.

Semaphore
    primitive process coordination mechanism.

Signal
    operation on a queue to restart a process.

Stable storage
    redundant memory system which preserves information even in the

event of a system failure.

Structured types
compound data types containing several elements, e.g. array and records.

Task
see Process.

Time-slicing
sharing the processor between several processes by executing each one for a short interval.

Transport service
interface between an application program an communication system.

Trap
special instruction that a program may use to request the services of the operating system.

Two phase commit
mechanism for implementing a distributed atomic transaction.

Virtual circuit
see connection oriented.

Wait
operation on a queue to suspend the current process.

References

Aho 1978
A. V. Aho and J. D. Ullman, *Principles of Compiler Design*, Addison Wesley, Reading, Mass. (1978).

Andrews 1977
G.R. Andrews and J. R. McGraw, "Language features for process interaction," in *Proc. ACM Conf. Language Design for Reliable Softw.: Raleigh N.C.* (March 1977).

Andrews 1981
G. R. Andrews, "Synchronizing Resources," *ACM Trans. Prog. Lang. Syst.* **3**(4) pp. 405-430 (Oct. 1981).

Andrews 1982
G. R. Andrews, "The distributed programming language SR- Mechanisms, design and implementation," *Softw. Pract. Exper.* **12**(8) pp. 719-754 (1982).

Barnes 1976
J. G. P. Barnes, *RTL/2: Design and philosophy*, Heyden, London (1976).

Bate 1986
G. Bate "Mascot 3: an Informal Introduction Tutorial," *Softw. Eng. J.* **1**(3) pp. 95-102 (May 1986).

Birrell 1982
A. D. Birrell, R. Levin, R. M. Needham, and M. D. Schroeder,

"Grapevine: an exercise in distributed computing," *Comm. ACM* **25**(4) pp. 260-74 (1982).

Birrell 1984
A. D. Birrell and B. J. Nelson, "Implementing Remote Procedure Calls," *ACM Trans. Comp. Syst.* **2**(1) pp. 39-59 (Feb 1984).

Bishop 1986
P. Bishop, *Fifth Generation Computers,* Ellis Horwood, Chichester, UK (1986).

Brinch Hansen 1973
P. Brinch Hansen, *Operating Systems Principles,* Prentice Hall, Englewood Cliffs N.J. (1973).

Brinch Hansen 1975
P. Brinch Hansen, "The programming language Concurrent Pascal," *IEEE Trans. Softw. Eng.* **SE-1**(2) pp. 199-206 (June 1975).

Brinch Hansen 1977
P. Brinch Hansen, *The Architecture of Concurrent Programs,* Prentice Hall, Englewood Cliffs (1977).

Brinch Hansen 1978
P. Brinch Hansen, "Distributed processes: A concurrent programming concept." *Commun. ACM* **21**(11) pp. 934-941 (Nov. 1978).

Buckley 1983
G. N. Buckley and A. Silberschatz, "An Effective Implementation of the Generalized Input-output Construct in CSP," *ACM Trans. Prog. Lang. Syst.* **5**(2) pp. 223-35 (April 1983).

Casey 1977
L.M. Casey, *Computer Structures for Distributed Systems,* Ph. D. Thesis, Edinburgh University (1977).

Chambers 1984
F.B. Chambers, D.A. Duce, and G.P. Jones, *Distributed Computing,* Academic Press, London (1984).

Cook 1980
R. Cook "*MOD- a Language for Distributed Programming," *IEEE Trans. Softw. Eng.* **SE-6** (6) pp. 563-71 (Nov 1980).

Date 1983
C. T. Date, *An Introduction to Database Systems, vol II* Addison-Wesley, Reading Mass. (1983).

Dijkstra 1968
E.W. Dijkstra, "Cooperating sequential processes," ed. F. Genuys in *Programming Languages* Academic Press, New York (1968).

Dijkstra 1975
E.W. Dijkstra, "Guarded commands, nondeterminancy and formal derivation of programs," *Commun. ACM* **18** (8) pp. 453-457 (Aug.

1975).

DoD 1983

DoD, *Reference manual for the Ada programming language,* U.S. Dept. of Defense, Washington (1983).

Dulay 1984

N. Dulay, J. Kramer, J. Magee, M. Sloman, and K. Twidle, *The Conic configuration language: doc 84/20* Imperial College, London (1984).

Eckhouse 1979

R. C. Eckhouse and L. R. Morris, *Mini Computer Systems* Prentice Hall, Englewood Cliffs (1979).

Farber 1972

D. J. Farber and K. C. Larson, "The System Architecture of the Distributed Computer System- the Communication System," in *Symp. Comput. Commun. Network and Teletraffic* pp. 21-27 (Apr. 1972).

Feldman 1979

J.A. Feldman, "High level programming for distributed computing," *Commun. ACM* **22** (6) pp. 353-368 (June 1979).

Grey 1979

J. N. Grey, "Notes on database operating systems," in *Operating systems: an advanced course* ed. G. Seegmuller, Springer-Verlag, New York (1979).

Gries 1971

D. Gries *Compiler construction for digital computers* Wiley, London (1971).

Hoare 1972

C. A. R. Hoare, "Proof of correctness of data representations," *Acta Informatica* **1** pp. 271-281 (1972).

Hoare 1974

C.A.R. Hoare, "Monitors: An operating system structuring concept," *Commun. ACM* **17** (10) pp. 549-557 (Oct. 1974).

Hoare 1978

C.A.R. Hoare, "Communicating sequential processes," *Commun. ACM* **21** (8) pp. 666-677 (Aug. 1978).

Hoare 1981

C. A. R. Hoare, "The Emporor's Old Cloths," *Comm. ACM* **23** (2) pp. 24-33 (1981).

Hoare 1985

C.A.R. Hoare, *Communicating Sequential Processes* Prentice Hall, Englewood Cliffs (1985).

Holt 1983

R. C. Holt, *Concurrent Euclid, the Unix operating system and Tunis* Addison Wesley, Reading Mass. (1983).

IEEE 1984
IEEE, *Token Ring Access Method and Physical Layer Specification: IEEE Standard 802.5* IEEE, New York, (Dec. 1984).

Inmos 1984
Inmos Ltd., *Occam programming manual* Prentice Hall, Englewood Cliffs, (1984).

Intel 1985
Intel Corp., *iAPX 286 Programmers' reference manual* Intel Corp., Santa Clara CA, (1985).

Jensen 1975
K. Jensen and N. Wirth *Pascal User Manual and Report* Springer-Verlag, New York (1975).

Kernighan 1978
B. W. Kernighan and D. M. Ritchie, *The C Programming Language* Prentice Hall, Englewood Cliffs (1978).

Kieburtz 1979
R. B. Kieburtz and A. Silberschatz, "Comments on Communicating Sequential Processes," *ACM Trans. Prog. Lang. Sys.* **1** (2) pp. 218-25 (1979).

King 1983
T. King and B. Knight, *Programming the M68000* Addison Wesley, London (1983).

Kramer 1983
J. Kramer, J. Magee, M. Sloman, and A. Lister, "Conic: An Integrated Approach to Distributed Computer Control Systems," *IEE Proc.* **130-E** (1) pp. 1-10 (Jan 1983).

Kramer 1984
J. Kramer, J. Magee, M. Sloman, K. Twidle, and N. Dulay, *The Conic programming language: doc 84/19* Imperial College, London (1984).

Lampson 1980
B.W. Lampson and D.D. Redell, "Experience with processes and monitors in Mesa," *Commun. ACM* **23** (2) pp. 105-117 (Feb. 1980).

Leblanc 1984
T. J. Leblanc, "The StarMod distributed programming kernel," *Softw. Pract. Exper.* **14** (12) pp. 1123-39 (1984).

Liskov 1983
B. Liskov and R. Scheifler, "Guardians and Actions: Linguistic Support for Robust Distributed Programs," *ACM Trans. Prog. Lang. Syst.* **5** (3) pp. 381-404 (July 1983).

May 1985
D. May and R. Shepherd, "Occam and the Transputer" ed. G.L. Reijns and E.L. Dagless, in *Concurrent Languages in Distributed Systems*

North Holland, Oxford (1985).

McQuillian 1977

J. M. McQuillian and D. C. Walden, "The ARPA network Design Decisions," *Computing Networks* **1** (Aug 1977).

Metcalf 1976

R.M. Metcalf and D.R. Boggs, "Ethernet - Distributed Packet Switching for Local Computer Networks," *Commun. ACM* **19** (7) pp. 395-404 (July 1976).

Needham 1983

R. M. Needham, A. J. Herbert, and J. B. Mitchell, "How to Connect Stable Memory to a Computer," *Operating Systems Review* **17** (1) (Jan. 1983).

Organick 1973

E. I. Organick, *Computer systems organization: B5700/B6700 series* Academic Press, New York (1973).

Pemberton 1982

S. Pemberton and M. Daniels *Pascal inmplementation: the P4 compiler and assemble/interpreter* Ellis Horwood, Chichester, UK (1982).

Raynal 1986

M. Raynal, *Algorithms for mutual exclusion* North Oxford Academic, London (1986).

Schroeder 1984

M. D. Schroeder, A. D. Birrell, and R. M. Needham, "Experience with Grapevine: the growth of a distributed system," *ACM Trans. Comput. Sys.* **2** (1) pp. 3-23 (1984).

Silberschatz 1977

A. Silberschatz, R. B. Kieburtz, and A. J. Bernstein, "Extending Concurrent Pascal to allow dynamic resource management," *IEEE Trans. Softw. Eng.* **SE-3** (3) pp. 210-17 (1977).

Silberschatz 1984

A. Silberschatz, "Cell: a distributed computing modularization concept," *IEEE Trans Softw. Eng.* **SE10**(2) pp. 178-184 (1984).

Spector 1982

A. Spector, "Performing Remote Operations on a Local Computer Network," *Comm. ACM* **25** (4) pp. 246-60 (1982).

Stratford-Collins 1982

M. J. Stratford-Collins, *ADA: a programmers conversion course* Ellis Horwood, Chichester, UK (1982).

Tanenbaum 1981

A.S. Tanenbaum, *Computer Networks* Prentice Hall, Englewood Cliffs N.J. (1981).

Thomas 1979
R. H. Thomas, "A Majority concensus approach to concurrency control for multiple copy databases," *ACM Trans. Database Sys.* **4** (2) pp. 180-209 (1979).

Verjus 1983
J-P. Verjus, "Synchronization in Distributed Systems - an informal introduction," in *Distributed computer systems* ed. Y. Parker and J-P. Verjus, Academic Press, (1983).

Welsh 1981
J. Welsh and A. Lister, "A comparative study of task communication in Ada," *Softw. Pract. Exper.* **11** pp. 256-290 (1981).

Whiddett 1983
R.J. Whiddett, "Dynamic Distributed Systems," *Softw. Pract. Exper.* **13** pp. 355-371 (1983).

Whiddett 1986
R.J. Whiddett, "Distributed Programs: An Overview of Implementations," *Microprocessors and Microsystems* **10** pp. 475-484 (1986).

Wilkes 1980
M.R. Wilkes and R.M. Needham, "The Cambridge Model Distributed System," *Oper. Syst. Rev.* **14** (21) (1980).

Wirth 1977a
N. Wirth, "Modula: A language for modular multi-programming," *Softw. Pract. Exper.* **7** pp. 3-35 (1977).

Wirth 1977b
N. Wirth, "The use of Modula," *Softw. Pract. Exper.* **7** pp. 37-65 (1977).

Wirth 1983
N. Wirth, "Programming in Modula-2: second edition," Springer-Verlag, New York (1983).

Woodward 1970
P. M. Woodward, P. R. Wetherall, and B. Gorman, *Official definition of Coral* HMSO, London (1970).

Young 1982
S. J. Young, *Real time languages: design and development* Ellis Horwood, Chichester, UK (1982).

Young 1984
S. J. Young, *An introduction to Ada* Ellis Horwood, Chichester, UK (1984).

Index